LIVING
THE GREAT
ADVENTURE

LIVING
THE GREAT
ADVENTURE

True stories of crisis
and discovery
from the pages of
FAITH AT WORK
selected and edited by
Richard Engquist

WORD BOOKS **WACO, TEXAS**

INTRODUCTION
■

With the passing of each day I become more convinced that the big failing of Christendom—of all of us who follow Him—lies in our rather ridiculous attempt to put God in a box: to confine Him to a particular church, a specific creed; to hem Him in, as it were, with our pet Scriptural interpretations; to decide how He will work in a given situation; to anthropomorphize Him.

There are no positive results from such attitudes on our part; there are only limiting consequences. God cannot be encased in our jargon, our religious emphases; He cannot be penned into our experiences or theories.

None of this is intended to imply that God is in any way changed by us. He *is* God and He *is* the same yesterday, today, and forever. Yet we have a distinct tendency to transform Him into our own inevitably distorted or minimized concepts. The Lord God never changes, but our experience with Him is surely governed by what He is like *to us*.

The adequacy or inadequacy of the Christian life is measurable by the accuracy or inaccuracy of our understanding of the nature of the God we follow. It is true that "no man has seen God at any time," but the Son has made Him known to us, and although no man can (in his mortal span) fully comprehend the nature of the Deity, anyone can, if he learns of Jesus Christ, learn of God. "I and the Father are one," Jesus declared, and I believe He made that declaration in order to relieve our confusion about what God, the Father, is really like.

God does not deal in the same way with any two persons. There is one common ground: the need for an initial turning by the human heart. But even there, He uses an infinite variety of ways to draw us by His Holy Spirit. No one of his own accord ever had the impetus to become a Christian. But the Spirit of God moves in ways so diverse, so creative—moves on the human heart in such wideness and scope as to stagger the most imaginative mind.

We cannot change God. It is God who changes us, and yet we can limit His activity toward us by the determined or careless effort to corner Him in our own airless concepts, slap our own little labels on Him and give the erroneous impression that He only acts this way or that. He has made it quite clear that His ways are higher than our ways, His thoughts than our thoughts. We tend to confine our witness to the story of our conversion. We confine our comfort-giving to trite, superficial statements about "everything being the will of God." We judge the spiritual state of our brother by the form of his baptism. We decide whether a person is a "true follower" by the lingo he uses to talk about God. We measure a man's dedication by whether he smokes or takes a drink or keeps a regular quiet time. How desperately we need to leave God free! We write and preach and chatter about how God frees us, and all the while we bind Him by refusing to permit the fresh air of His true nature in Christ to blow through our stuffy religious notions.

The clean, fresh air of God blows through this collection of true stories, *Living the Great Adventure*. God is here permitted to be Himself, to work through His Holy Spirit. Each person shares discoveries from his time of crisis. In one sense, these are all conversion stories, but they are not all stories of initial conversion. Life is a series of conversions if it is a life of adventure with God. There is no such thing as standing still in the consciousness of the Father's presence. We are either fleeing Him or moving ahead. And we move ahead according to how free we are within the Christian family to be ourselves and to follow a God who is also left free to be Himself with us.

New life in Christ is no longer a taboo subject socially. When I first turned to Him eighteen years ago it was. Shortly after my conversion, I spoke at a large and respected theological seminary. I did not make a theological speech because I did not know how. I simply witnessed to the adventure and reality of my new life in Christ. When I had finished, two earnest, scholarly young seminarians approached me with puzzled expressions on their faces. "Just what," they asked, "do you believe really happened to you?" I tried to tell them as simply as possible, and suddenly one of them interrupted: "Oh, I know! You've got first century Christianity!"

Anyone who has been touched by the life of God has first century Christianity. Those first Christians shared and re-shared one shining piece of news: "The Lord is risen!" The early Christians never tired of the telling. Jesus Christ, their Master, had gotten up and walked out of His tomb! This was the most exciting, the most vital experience of their lives. The knowledge that they did not follow merely a great man who died for them changed them utterly. They followed a risen, living Lord who would be living *for* them forever.

Forced sharing even about Christ is worthless. When one shares Him because one can't keep still, life is shared. Life is shared in the simple stories here, and the variety of experience is striking. Faith at Work is, so far as I know, the freest fellowship available to followers of Jesus Christ.

Living the Great Adventure is a collection of experiences told by people who do not try to impress us with their own spirituality. One man asked God to prove Himself by giving him a winner at the race track! These are honest narratives, from honest minds, and any reader can identify with at least one of the experiences in these pages. They toot no denominational horns. They speak of man's need and God's supply. You will not find God bound here—you will find Him free to set men free. God is glorified, not those who tell their stories. Some of the personalities are more dramatic than others, but all are *living the great adventure* within, where the Spirit of the living God has come to stay.

Eugenia Price

St. Simons Island, Georgia
April, 1967

FOREWORD

Some of us fear change, but change is inevitable. To say, "I am what I am, and nothing can be done about it," is both unrealistic and futile.

The question is not, "Can I change?" but, "How am I changing and where am I going?" Every dead end in life can be a turning point.

This book contains factual accounts of incidents and events in the lives of many people. They are people from a variety of backgrounds, representing a wide range of temperament and attitudes.

In one respect, however, they are similar. Each describes changes in his life—changes precipitated by crisis, desperation, dissatisfaction, anguish, or mere boredom. The authors use terms such as "decision," "release," "surrender,"—even "conversion." Readers will decide for themselves what these terms mean in specific cases, and whether they have a wider application.

But we feel safe in making one prediction: If you read these true personal stories, you cannot avoid the conclusion that here are individuals who have moved from the dreary experience of "death in life" to something quite different. For here are men and women who are *living the great adventure.*

All of these stories first appeared in the magazine FAITH AT WORK, under the editorship of Irving Harris and Walden Howard. People who read such stories often say, "Great! But does it last?" For this reason we have selected narratives which have stood the test of time. A few lines following each story give some of the "here and now" of the various authors.

At the same time, people are not building blocks, staying in a fixed position until the wrecking crew appears. In presenting these stories, we have nothing to prove. The experiences are retold for whatever they are worth. The facts speak for themselves.

Richard Engquist

Associate Editor
Faith at Work
New York, N.Y.
October, 1967

CONTENTS

■

PART ONE
■

TURNING POINTS

Crisis comes in many forms: the unexpected stab of pain, the loss of a loved one, the failure of a marriage, the realization that existence seems pointless, the admission of defeat.

These first stories describe crises in the lives of individuals. Some are dramatic, some prosaic, but each becomes a decisive turning point. Is one of these "your story?" Does it point to an option you have failed to take into account?

Do you find yourself responding positively to these unvarnished snatches of autobiography, or do you become suspicious? Read on . . .

Chapter 1

■

ACCOUNT RENDERED

by Gert Behanna
Author of *The Late Liz*

As far back as I can remember, I was told I was the master of my fate. I got so I really believed it. I finally came to believe I was the master of the fate of a lot of other people, too. I was "a born leader;" only plenty of times, others didn't want to be led, so I'd push them.

I knew all the answers. Many people resented that; but, when they did, this just proved how ungrateful they were.

If I talked hard enough, long enough, I usually floored them —inundated them with words. My ego relished this. I'd won! And I actually thought I *had* won—thought others were convinced, when they were finally silenced. But they weren't merely silent; before long they were absent.

Of course, sometimes I did help people; I'm not a monster. I've often spent time doing things for others which were right and fine and appeared unselfish. But those deeds weren't done for the right reasons. They were done for me.

Finally, the self-justification and the self-love ran out. They had to. There wasn't the slightest proof anywhere that I was indispensable. Everyone was fed up with my excellence. But even when I got to the bottom rung, *saw* what had happened and *why,* my pride wasn't licked. Oh, no! Self-pity took over

then, and that was the worst of all. Tears practically drowned
that poor old Inner Voice, and I really hit bottom.

Sick with self-distaste, I knew I was licked, but nowhere—not
anywhere—was there a remedy. The despair and loneliness, the
agonies of humiliation and hysteria, the final utter desperation
did not come all at once. They were forced on me by a ghastly
personal crisis in my life. The total account was finally rendered.
Then I even tried to pray.

I'd always given some lip-service to God. I'd always inferred
I believed in Someone. I'd believed in Him in about the way a
young person anticipates, in the distant future, an old-age pen-
sion. I didn't go to church, but some day I did think I'd get
around to going, give God my patronage.

If you don't mind a few clinical facts, I'm going to tell you
what my "tests" showed about them. They showed a middle-
aged woman dangerously close to a mental breakdown. My
blood pressure was 187, the red blood-count was under three
million (five million is normal), the hemoglobin was forty-two!
And, just for good measure, the colon was spastic. "You'd better
take a vacation, Mrs. Behanna, you need an entire change." I
certainly did! So I went to friends in Connecticut. I wept on
their shoulders and told them how misunderstood I was, how
difficult others made my life. It wasn't a vacation for them, I
can assure you!

Then, one evening in July, my hostess told me about two
guests who were coming for dinner. Their names were Tom and
Blanche Page, she said, and I'd like them. They'd had a "wonderful" experience awhile back, it seemed—they'd been "converted" and it had changed their whole lives.

Converted! Revival meetings—dirt floors—shouting—corn-
ball songs. And here they were, coming to dinner and in New
Canaan, too! In my circle, God wasn't considered socially *au
fait;* but I do remember that I was more than curious.

If you knew Tom and Blanche, you could imagine my amazement. No fanatic's look about those two. Nothing smug or complacent. Just charming and normal and casual.

Even now, long after we've all laughed about it, I get pretty squirmy when I recall how I barraged them belligerently with my problems. On and on, to those gentle strangers, I ranted of my difficulties with others, how hard, stupid, or indifferent they were! If only the world would listen to Gert, how much better off we'd be. I think I even brought in the Almighty. Wow!

The Pages listened—and then it happened. Tom turned and asked quietly, "Why don't you turn all this over to God?" That's all. He slipped it in gently, even with a little humor, but it literally staggered me. It was my introduction to the simplicity of God.

I stared at him. Finally I gasped, "You say that as though I had heavy suitcases and needed a porter." Tom nodded. "That's about it," he said.

The rest of the evening is hazy; yet I do know that for the first time in years I was out of the driver's seat.

Ten days later I drove back to Illinois. The little question drove back with me: "Why don't you turn all this over to God?" It didn't make sense, of course, but then a melody doesn't make sense either.

Tom had made it sound so simple and I was so very, very sick of me. Sick of battling my conscience; sick of hurting and being hurt; finally even sick of running things. But God—where was God? Even if you *wanted* to turn things over to Him, how did you do it? Somewhere inside, a rusty old door was beginning to creak open—just a little.

When I reached home, I found a mass of mail. I also found a letter from the Pages, a magazine, a small booklet called *Faith That Works*. My memory is vivid as to what happened then. I tossed the other mail aside and read their letter and a warm

glow went through my heart. Here, again, was that same simplicity. They wrote about God as though He were a mutual
friend whom they had seen more recently than I. And what
overwhelmed me was their word that they were praying for me!
It sounded practical and efficient, like calling the doctor. I felt
grateful and a little humble, but, being me, *I* wanted to call Him
myself. How did you do that?

I opened the magazine and read Sam Shoemaker's "Before
It Is Too Late," and then in *Faith That Works* I read Horace
Lukens' "How To Love People." That was it! Within twenty
minutes it was all over.

No one, certainly not I, can describe the beauty of a rainbow
or an evening star. How, then, can one put into words the forgiveness of God! I only know that right there and then the dam
burst. Within twenty mortal minutes, the self-important Gert
capitulated. God moved in.

He didn't find His new house neat and shiny. But He did find
a welcome. Lots of old furnishings have been thrown out since
then. Some have been re-done. (With unbelievable generosity
other people are helping me to find new pieces which will be
"fittin'.") The "grounds" of His new house are still overgrown
with tough old weeds and harsh brambles. But, with constant
daily work and patience, with constant help from God and
people, the sun and rain and wind are getting through. The soil
is beginning to sweeten.

I have so much help now. Of course, there are tons of tough
problems—make no mistake about that. There are sticklers
like this: Am I being proud of not being proud? Is my desire to
talk about God a new form of exhibitionism? When I don't
know, I shut up—I shut up and go to the Bible, or some other
good book. I am ready to ask God *His* way. And sooner or later
He tells me.

If this account seems vague and nebulous, if this "club" seems hard to join, let me suggest what I've found to be the basic house rules. I've found just three: Face yourself. Really love God. And then *prove* it. They all dovetail. If I don't love myself, if I do love God, I *will* prove it.

The rules are simple, but living up to them is not. As I said, old habits are the very dickens to break. And the old gent with the gay, red suit and the cold eyes still hovers around. But now I recognize him. He's increasingly disgruntled, too.

And now I know my goal. I used to fight myself *for* myself and didn't know what I wanted. Now I am fighting myself for God and I've got a pretty good idea of what *He* wants. Nothing wrong with a good fight when you're sure of the cause. In different words my rules are: first need Him, then love Him, then prove it.

The actual crisis which began all this is far from being "righted." How could it be? It took years to bring about. But that's no longer my business—it's God's. He'll decide the final issue and that's all right with me. I'm completely content to leave everything in His hands, no matter how His decisions turn out. In the meantime, I have a full-time job—pulling weeds.

P.S. Oh, yes, my health's so good I almost forgot to bring you up to date. My new Physician took care of all that in about six weeks. The blood pressure is normal, the red blood count is normal, the hemoglobin is ninety-four! As to the "innards"— they're just fine, thanks!   —*June, 1948*

In 1966 I met Gert Behanna for the first time—some eighteen years after she wrote this account of her conversion. In the intervening period she had published a best-selling autobiography, The Late Liz, *which appeared under the pseudonym Elizabeth Burns; she had recorded two widely-distributed albums, and filled literally thousands of speaking engagements. As a FAITH AT WORK editor I had had some correspondence with Gert, but nothing had prepared me for the electric quality of her personality, the keenness of her mind, the depth of her faith, or the charisma of her presence. These cannot be captured in words. "Newsweek" tried, in reporting her precedent-shattering sermon from the chapel pulpit at Yale University (she was the first woman to invade that lofty rostrum). Fortunately, through personal appearances and recordings, she has put "flesh" on the skeleton of her life story, and her impact will not soon be forgotten. Gert Behanna is certainly one of the amazing personalities of our generation.*

Chapter 2

■

"HOME, JAMES!"

by Donald T. James
Director, The Pittsburgh Experiment

World War II was in full swing. During my senior year in high school I enlisted in the Marine Corps, wanting to die and figuring this was the best way to do it. My father had died when I was fourteen, and my mother three years later. After that, I didn't have much use for life.

For three years I was navigator-bombardier in the Pacific on special assignments. Our squadron flew B-25's on twelve-hour night missions. The strategy was to fly one plane at a time from Saipan to the Japanese mainland with ships strung out beneath to pick us up if necessary. We carried rockets but no guns, and no protection except for flying at low altitudes, about fifty feet above the water. Our record of loses was sixty percent.

One night we were on a mission when home base radioed to inform us that we were just five minutes away from a hurricane. The pilot called me for a heading home, and I had a chance to shoot just one star, which indicated winds of 125 miles an hour, blowing in our faces. I refused to believe it, and estimated a new heading at ninety miles an hour.

There was a checkpoint of rocks 125 miles south of Japan. I estimated our time of arrival, but when we were due, no rocks were in sight. Radar didn't pick up a thing. We were a hundred feet above water, with waves now thirty or forty feet high. The crew was violently ill.

The pilot asked, "Are you sure you know what you're doing?" Holding a rag over my mouth and working with one hand, I answered, "Don't worry. We'll make it, but we may be late."

He turned the intercom on so everyone could hear, and said to the crew, "I don't think this damn navigator knows what he's doing."

I replied over the intercom that if he didn't like what I was doing he could navigate himself, adding that the minute he took over I would quit and would not be responsible for what happened. After five minutes he took over, and I turned off my light, climbed up on the navigation table and sat down. Just then the radio man hollered that the rocks were underneath. The pilot called, "Home, James!"

That night there was dead silence on the field as we went to our tents. After we had been questioned by the intelligence people, a routine procedure, the co-pilot said to me, "I think you need a drink." We sat on the front steps of his tent and killed a fifth of liquor, but we couldn't get drunk. I realized that the pilot and I would never fly together again, for we didn't trust each other. It worked out that he and I both requested a transfer; his was granted and I stayed with the crew.

At last the war was over and I went home. I'd wanted to die, but I was still alive.

My time was pretty well taken up with fun and games. Once or twice a year I would go to church when my sister forced me— usually having to wake me from a drunken stupor.

But when I met Joan and fell in love, life looked different. We both wanted children, and we wanted to become members of a church. Joan was a Roman Catholic, and we worked out a "deal": we would visit a different church each Sunday until we found one that was acceptable to both of us.

It didn't work. After three weeks of marriage Joan couldn't bring herself to go into another church. Most nights she cried herself to sleep.

Even though our "deal" had fallen through, I felt compelled to go to church each Sunday. The only strength I had to draw on was what I remembered from my mother and the clergyman I had known as a child. I kept trying to imagine what they would tell me to do if they were still alive. The thought came strong and clear that I should ask God's guidance for handling the situation. It was too much for the self-sufficient Don James to cope with.

Joan and I were out drinking most Saturday nights, but amazingly, whether drunk or sober, I would wake on Sunday and go to church. This went on for six months.

Then one Sunday I sat down in an Episcopal church and a lady next to me turned, told me her name, and asked whether I was "new" there. During the six months I had been wandering from church to church, no one had spoken to me, and after the initial shock I said, "Yes Ma'am, this is my first time here."

"Our service may be strange to you," she said. "If you like, I will be happy to lead you so that it might have more meaning for you."

What that woman triggered was fantastic. When the service was over she offered to take me to the Parish House for a coffee hour, and to introduce me to some people my own age. All this friendliness was a bit frightening, so I told the woman my wife was ill and I had to go home.

Next Sunday I went back—the first time I had ever revisited a church. And I kept going back. This made Joan curious, and she wanted to go with me. For a month we attended together, and then decided we wanted to join the church. The rector advised us to wait six months before joining; he wanted to make sure this was the last change we would ever make.

At this point I was feeling quite proud of myself. Not only was I going to church but I had "converted" my Roman Catholic wife! At the time this seemed a great accomplishment.

The rector invited us to join a group of young married couples to review a book, *How To Become a Christian*. I thought, *Well, this will be a good thing—for Joan.*

Shortly I found out that Joan had more faith in her little finger than I had in my whole being. For the first three weeks of the six-week course I felt smug about being nice to my wife; then I realized that *I* was the one who needed to learn how to be a Christian.

When the course ended, the rector suggested that those of us who were interested should continue to meet as a small discussion-and-prayer group. This met weekly, and became the second such group of what was eventually to become the Pittsburgh Experiment. There were six couples, and two of the men are now in the ministry.

A year later we moved to a new community. We were disappointed in the church there, so we began "commuting" on Sundays to our parish in the city. When the rector cornered us and asked what we were doing there, I told him we didn't like the church in our neighborhood. He said we were wrong, and if we persisted in coming back he would throw us out. He also informed me that the minister I did not like was interested in starting prayer-discussion groups and that we should offer our experience to him.

We did so, and the group which resulted eventually grew into three groups. Out of them has come one minister, one missionary pilot, and four men who now serve as trustees of the Pittsburgh Experiment. Three couples moved to other cities and have started prayer groups in their new neighborhoods.

During our second year in the new community, I thought about going into the ministry. I really wanted to do it. Meanwhile, our family had grown to the point where we needed a house, and my sister and brother-in-law offered us their home at a fantastically low price—almost a gift.

In September, 1958, I went to a men's retreat at St. Barnabas Home in Gibsonia. Most of the time was to be spent in meditation. During the first period of meditation I was kneeling on flagstone, praying but feeling most uncomfortable. I looked up at a rugged wooden cross which hung above the altar, and prayed for strength to kneel for just a few minutes. "Lord, I know you hung on that cross for three hours. Help me to kneel for just a few minutes and bear the discomfort." Then I thought, *This is it—the time to enter the ministry.* The idea persisted during the entire meditation. Even taking a long walk around the grounds did not help me to shake it.

After the second meditation I went to my minister and told him of my thoughts. He suggested I continue to pray and ask for God's guidance as to whether this was valid or merely something I had dreamed up. By the time the retreat ended there was no doubt in my mind.

I wondered how I could summon the courage to tell Joan. We had three children. For the first time we had a nice home, and things were going pretty well for me in the insurance business. Only recently it had been decided that if my work continued to go well, I would be sent to the home office in the training department within a year.

To say the least, Joan was not happy with my decision. All she could think of was how hard we had worked to get where we were, and how I was going to throw it all away to start something which held no guarantee of a secure future, materially speaking. We prayed together, and finally realized there was nothing to do but trust the Lord regarding the future.

Bishop Austin Pardue interviewed me for three hours. He decided my call was valid and that I should try to enter the Epis-

copal Theological Seminary in Lexington, Kentucky. But it was
the end of September, and classes had already been in session for
two weeks. I went to Lexington to talk with Bishop Moody, head
of the seminary, and to have a psychiatric examination.

The Bishop decided that if I could clear up my business, sell
my house (we needed the money), and return within three
weeks, he would give me a chance to catch up in the work I had
missed.

When I told my employer what I was trying to do, he fired
me. This put a real kink in our finances, but I couldn't help
feeling that it was God's will to force me to take quick action.

Almost miraculously, we sold the house fast, for cash, at a high
price. And so, within three weeks, I was in Lexington.

After all that has happened to us, Joan and I believe firmly
that God does have a job for us to do, and that He will continue
to give us whatever strength is necessary.   —*December, 1961*

*A flashing grin, a colorful vocabulary, seemingly inexhaustible
energy, and profound gifts as a spiritual leader: these combine to
make Don James a unique force in lay renewal in and around
Pittsburgh. Also prominent among his assets are a lovely wife
and a bunch of lively kids.*

*The impact of the Pittsburgh Experiment has been enormous,
largely because of Don's leadership. I have been privileged to
see him "in action" a number of times: hammering home practical truths from a platform, skillfully drawing out men in a talk-it-
over group, combining horse-sense leadership with breathtaking
vision at a meeting of contemporary "prophets." But the thing
I will always remember most vividly about Don is that once
when we happened to share a hotel room, he knelt down in his
pajamas by the side of his bed, simply and unashamedly, and
said his prayers before retiring. Power on its knees is always
affecting, for it testifies to the Source of the power.*

Chapter 3

∎

OUT OF DARKNESS

by Marjorie Perley
Housewife, South March, Ontario

I stood on the steps of a large house in a major Canadian city. It was a blustery March evening some years ago, and the weather without mirrored the confusion I felt within. I was about to attend a "fireside meeting"—but *why?* What was I doing here?

For that matter, what was I doing *anywhere?* Life had lost its meaning; nothing seemed very clear or important—yet I was only twenty-two years old.

Finally I rang the doorbell, and a roomful of young people welcomed me. It was an evening full of shocks, beginning with what was revealed about the story in the third chapter of the Gospel of John. I thought I knew that chapter, but the way the leader presented it—with intense reality—was something new.

Moreover, this man reflected a personal quality that I could not pinpoint, but which was extremely attractive. The girl who had invited me possessed this quality also. As I looked about, I could see it in the faces of others. Phrases like "new life" and "made over" kept ringing in my ears, piercing my confusion and depression. . . .

New life! That was what I'd meant to find when I left England and emigrated to Canada. Surely with new surroundings, happier circumstances, a different home, I could expect much—

27

but the trouble was that I'd brought the "old me" right along.

A surge of self-pity went through me as I thought again of "home." It was a small town in Bedfordshire—an ordinary town—and ours was an ordinary house, but with anything but an ordinary atmosphere!

I was an only child, and ever since I could remember my father and I had been at odds. Through the years our differences had been magnified until my resentment almost reached the point of hatred. On the other hand, I deeply loved my mother.

During the war years Father was overseas, and Mother and I became almost like sisters. We did everything together, and it seemed to me that life was very pleasant. Then with the war's end Father returned, and my world fell apart again.

At sixteen I tried to act grown up, but to my father I was just a rebellious teen-ager. His attempts to make me into a dutiful daughter were not intentionally domineering, but he was bewildered by my coldness and convinced that severe discipline was the remedy.

I spent more and more time alone, withdrawing into myself, nursing my resentment and bitterness and thinking only of escape. Then, late in 1946, my chance came. One winter morning I left England for Canada, vowing never to return. In spite of my love for Mother, I was glad to cut myself off from everything connected with the old life.

But life in Canada did not fulfill my vision, though I loved the country. I could not understand this, and my old hatred for Father seemed to deepen. Still, I was determined to make a go of things. I soon found a job, then a better one.

Then one obstacle after another arose—most of them physical. A medical report showed that I had a heart murmur, and along with this news came some recurring skin trouble. I became greatly depressed, and because of medical bills my bank account dwindled steadily. My ailments, I believed, stemmed from a constant state of tension, and I delved into psychology in a desperate attempt to understand and get control of myself and my increasing fears. Visits to a psychiatrist followed. Talking things out with this kindly man gave temporary relief, but his advice seemed trite and unworkable. "There's nothing wrong with your mind," he said (though I had begun to doubt this). "Just forget yourself and lose yourself in others."

I knew I needed something more than this, yet I tried to follow his suggestions. First as president of a young people's group, then in Presbytery activities, I became deeply involved in meetings, committees, and projects. My tension only increased. It was as if I were running away from something, not daring to stop and think out what it was. I lay awake nights, full of the old feelings and fears. When I tried to pray, I felt that it was useless and that God Himself couldn't help me. I had just been "born wrong."

One night I sat on the edge of my bed and the terrible feeling swept over me that I could not go on. There was a bottle of disinfectant in my hand and I was trying to get up the courage to drink it. I remember lifting the bottle to my mouth, and then thinking of what such an act would mean to the family I was living with. This thought—or so I believed at the time—was the only thing that stopped me.

Shortly afterward, while struggling to appear normal and calm, I attended a Christian rally and after the meeting found myself talking to someone about full-time service in the Church. It seems ludicrous now, but I had to have something to work toward, and church work was taking much of my time anyway. Finally the girl, whom I scarcely knew, invited me to go to a "fireside group meeting" with her. And there I was, that March evening. . . .

One by one young people in that room talked about Jesus and

what He meant to them personally. They represented many denominations, and together they made a strong appeal.

Among those attending, and unnoticed by me that first night, was my future husband. One of the girls who spoke attracted me especially, and together we talked till midnight, long after the meeting had ended. When I realized at last that it was a Person I needed so desperately, our talk ended with a prayer and an unreserved offering of myself to Jesus Christ.

"My life is a mess," I told God. "You take it from here, please." I gave Him my past, present, and future, and asked Him to come in and be my Lord.

Christ performed a sudden operation on the deep cancer of hatred within me. Suddenly it was gone. For the first time I felt clean inside—I felt *free*. It was like a wonderful dream come true.

After that beginning there was much to learn and much to unlearn. I had to try to love, and let God love through me. As He showed me more of the meaning of the cross, there came awareness of specific sins. There was restitution to make, letters to write, resentments to confess and ask forgiveness for. But the joy, the freedom in losing myself in the things of God, the inward peace that Jesus brought into my life were worth infinitely more than the hard knocks to my pride. Soon I knew the thrill of a good night's sleep and, a bit later, the blessing of a completely sound body. My skin trouble disappeared, and my doctor declared my heart completely normal and healthy again.

Then, a year later, God led me to do the very thing I had vowed I would never do—go back to England on a visit. I had been away for five years, and it was with some trembling as well as trusting that I sailed. But a family crisis had arisen, I was needed, and God told me to go.

How He triumphed! My parents and friends stared, and I certainly couldn't blame them. I was definitely different. When the opportunity came for me to speak for a few minutes in a Salvation Army Hall, telling how Jesus had changed my life, bewilderment was written on my mother's face—but it proved the prelude to her entrance into the same "new life" the following day.

The crisis was resolved, the new relationship between my father and me became a thing of constant wonder, and I returned to Canada some weeks later much poorer financially, but infinitely richer in faith.

Again and again I have found God's grace sufficient for my every need. I have made mistakes, had disappointments great and small, and found some things hard to understand; but always in Jesus Christ I have been made whole, and I can only proclaim in wonder that He has truly called me out of darkness into His marvelous light.   —*January, 1960*

Post Script: Through a series of misunderstandings and personal difficulties, I lost my sense of balance, and in 1963 suffered a mental breakdown. For twenty-four hours my sanity was lost to me. As the doctor put it bluntly to me later, "You were on the very threshold—you just didn't go through."

I knew Who had prevented this, and as I came out of the terrible darkness, somewhere deep within it seemed the Lord was telling me, "Love is the only answer."

Later I came to realize that the destructive emotions related in my story had "gone underground," even though I felt consciously free of them. As resentment and bitterness were piled on top of the backlog, the pot boiled over and I lost control.

Although there was much suffering involved, perhaps especially for my young son, I can find myself able to say now that I am thankful it happened. God's hand was definitely in all that happened to me to bring about a deeper healing, and I can only trust Him to work it out for good to others who were involved. God gave me the grace—and is still giving it—to accept and find myself in a completely new way.   —*April, 1967*

Marjorie Perley's story came to the FAITH AT WORK editorial office as an unsolicited manuscript. The authenticity of her experience was immediately apparent, and it was subsequently corroborated by mutual friends in Canada. The fireside group which she describes existed for many years in Ottawa in the home of Mr. and Mrs. Robert Fraser. Miracles took place in that setting, where dozens of young people found not only new life but vocations in the Church and in various avenues of service to the world. Bob and Muriel Fraser have taken flight from "this mortal coil," but their faith, vision, and zeal live on in individuals like Marjorie Perley and hundreds of others all over the world.

Chapter 4

■

GRANDSTAND PLAY

by Perry Storm
Law Department Employee, Railroad Company
Albany, New York

One hot August Saturday, in the bumper-to-bumper traffic on the road to Saratoga, I asked God to prove His existence by giving me a sign. His answer came so quickly and surely as to rock me to the bottom of my soul, and gave me the spark of faith I needed to turn my life inside out.

For forty-four years I had been crawling slowly upward toward the light of belief in God, only to lose my grip time after time. August of 1959 found me frustrated in business, confused in family relationships, tired in body and soul.

It's not that I was ignorant of Christianity. In fact, my father had taught me how to read by using the Bible as a textbook and the 28th chapter of Matthew as my lesson. How he glowed with pride when, by the light of a kerosene lamp, I groped my way to the final verse.

But ten days after my sixth birthday my father was lowered into the ground at the feet of a widow and four little children. From that unmarked grave—we cannot find it now—distrust was planted in me.

Nine years in a home for fatherless boys did little to increase

33

my faith. Rules were enforced with a heavy razor-strop; love was experienced only at intervals when a boy went home for a visit—if he had a home; schooling was geared to the necessity of earning a living beginning the moment we completed the equivalent of a high school course.

"Success" was the goal held up to us: an indefinite combination of making money, seeking position, and attaining power. Against this background the weekly chapel assembly and the hour-long Sunday service, with "successful" businessmen, politicians, educators, and other influential people substituting for clergymen, brought me no nearer to God. At seventeen several of us boys boasted of our atheism. And yet, through the years, a fragment of a hymn by James Russell Lowell haunted me at intervals:

> *". . . and behind the dim unknown,*
> *Standeth God within the shadow,*
> *Keeping watch above His own."*

After graduation I acquired a good job and an automobile, and with ample money in my pocket I could follow an around-the-clock schedule of wine, women, and song. Then an auto accident left me with such a horribly scarred face that I hid in my room night after night asking, "Is there a God?" During that period I read the Bible from cover to cover.

Thirty years later I found myself with an unhappy wife, four children, five grandchildren, a fairly good job, a mortgaged home, a few friends, and the same unanswered question.

By then I realized that success, wealth, power, and position had eluded me. Worse than that, I had not found the happiness which I assumed was a by-product of those things.

Through the years, as an example to the children and because it was the thing to do, I had been a member of a church, but

I knew I was a professing and not a practicing Christian though I attended services regularly and even taught Sunday school.

I had persuaded myself that there must be a Creator and Maintainer of the universe, but I could not be convinced that there was a God who cared about individuals. To me, Jesus Christ was a man whose teachings spelled out an ideal way of life, but belief in His resurrection, or the conviction that He was alive in the world today, were hurdles I could not surmount.

I had the good fortune to meet a minister who seemed able to make Christianity work. Cautiously, over many months, I discussed my problems with him. One day I blurted out, "I just don't have *any* faith!"

He explained that a man can get faith by sharing in experiences of faith with others who have it. He urged me to join a Saturday morning breakfast group of men who were practicing faith at work. For weeks I attended—not speaking but listening with increased interest to discussions of prayers answered, problems solved, lives changed.

Meanwhile I met a rugged police chief who told me matter-of-factly that he had stopped smoking through prayer while teaching a Sunday school class of convicts in New York State's worst prison; that he had been cured of cancer; that he had spent years trying to disprove the Bible, only to be converted to absolute belief in Jesus Christ.

I started to pray for strength to stop smoking—without results. I also prayed vainly for help in solving a worsening domestic problem. Finally I told the police chief that I wanted to believe, I had tried hard to believe, but that I simply could not. To my surprise he grinned and said confidently, "That's fine! Now you're ready. If you're not straining to believe all by yourself, God can prove His existence to you. Pray for something and see what happens. *Dare to do it.*" Still grinning, he walked away.

These words came back to me that hot August day as I was driving to Saratoga. My wife and daughter and I were on our way to the racetrack. Creeping along in a line of traffic, slowed by a construction project, I had plenty of time to think.

Did I dare to ask God to give me faith? Well, what did I have to lose? Despite my efforts, by myself I had not been successful. What's more, I had no particular desire to go on living another fifteen or twenty years if the future held nothing more than the past.

And then a wild, improbable idea entered my head. It was so wacky that at first I dismissed it—but then I remembered that my friend had said, "God keeps surprising us. With Him nothing is improbable."

The wild idea was this: that God would prove Himself to me by giving me a winner at the racetrack! This was about as far from conventional "religious experience" as anything I could imagine, yet for the first time in memory I was suddenly at peace. The crawling cars and the honking horns no longer jangled on my nerves.

In a kind of reverie I seemed to become aware of decisions that needed to be made: I must decide to let God take charge of my life. I must ask forgiveness for every sin I had ever committed, and, in turn, I must forgive every wrong anyone had ever done me. I must keep still and listen. I must keep "in tune" with God, through the long afternoon and forever after.

As I definitely accepted these ideas, the feeling of peace remained.

Finally we arrived at the grandstand, and through eight races I remained serene and rather detached. Then, just before the last race, something stirred within me. I was oddly excited. The conviction came that Jesus Christ, a living Spirit, was right there —that He was everywhere, even at a racetrack.

The conviction was so strong that my former notion that He would prove His existence by giving me a winning horse seemed suddenly very silly. But it seemed as if God had determined to prove to me—as to doubting Thomas—that He cared enough about me to shatter completely the bonds of my unbelief.

My wife and I put some money on a horse. It was neither a favorite nor a long shot, but at the announcer's words, "They're off!" I knew our horse would win. It got off to a discouraging start, back in the pack at the back stretch, and hopelessly behind at the far turn. Then it happened! The announcer's voice, usually icily calm, became excited. A horse was coming from behind, swinging out around all the others, winging its way home. Sure enough, our horse had caught the leaders and, flying by the grandstand, he was way out in front and sure to win, going away. He was the most decisive winner of the day. At that moment I was so overwhelmed with awe that my hair seemed to stand on end.

Well, no man leaps from sinner to saint in an instant, and in the months since that experience at the racetrack I, too, have had ups and downs. Still I am working it out, at home, at church, on the job, in fellowship groups.

Here are some of the key things I have found about growing in faith: *pray thankfully,* accepting and granting forgiveness; *be still* and know that God is God—and that all other gods (power, material things, etc.) are false; *seek first the kingdom*—let God take over and He will arrange your life better than you ever could yourself; *drop your burdens* at the cross, without holding anything back—Jesus will come alive in your heart and give you joy; *share your experiences* of faith with others; *claim the power* that God gives—love can accomplish anything; *dare to speak up* for the Master in all things—it is harder to be a Christian in all one's acts, and tell men so, than to profess but not practice it.

My one regret is that it took me fifty years to learn what the thief on the cross grasped in minutes. The difference was a crucified Christ—he saw Him then, I have found Him only now.

—*May, 1960*

Tough, bright, jolly, with a sentimental streak, Perry Storm reminds me of the Horatio Alger heroes many of us admired as children. Through sheer force of will he rose above a childhood which was like something out of a melodrama, and he slugged it out in a man's world. But what makes Perry unique and delightful is a spiritual dimension. I met him and his charming wife Mabel shortly after this story appeared in FAITH AT WORK magazine, and told him that some of our readers couldn't swallow the fact that he found God at a racetrack. Perry just grinned. He realized that God is much bigger than all our conceptions of Him, and much more surprising. He simply told his story "like it was."

Chapter 5

■

ANOTHER LIFE FOR JOAN

by Joan Gibbons
Fashion Model, London, England*

Chin up, Joan. Never admit failure. These phrases sum up an attitude, typical of many British people, which has characterized most of my life. Even as a child I was selfish, strong-willed, and full of pride. Recklessly I rushed into an early marriage, perhaps because my parents forbade me to do so.

It did not take long to realize what a mistake this was, but Joan knew everything and would not dream of asking for help or advice. Two children were born, but the marriage was a failure and finally ended in divorce.

Then, immediately, another marriage, to a charming man I loved with all my heart. There followed seven agonizing years, for he was weak and sweet and couldn't say no to a drink. No human love could save us, and at last I divorced him, too. Shortly afterward he died, and I felt that my world had fallen apart.

But would I admit it? Never! I was completely wretched, physically ill, but still it was "chin up." A strong will and pride somehow kept me going.

---

*At the time this story was written, the author lived in New York City.

Now, for the first time, I was faced with the necessity of having to earn a living. I'd had everything—maids, cars, chauffeurs, plenty of money—all the things that are supposed to make us happy but never do. Now all was gone, and here was Joan, who had always been sure she could do anything for herself, actually on her own. And now I began to find out what worry really was.

Someone offered me a job in America—a good but demanding job. For five years I traveled throughout the States, until the Bank of England said, "No more dollars," and the job came to an end.

During this period I, too, was coming to an end. Constantly worried and fearful, I made myself so ill that within four years I had four major operations. At one point I was in hospital for over three months, and nearly died.

Then someone suggested that I become a model, and though it seemed an incredible idea at my age, I was willing to try anything. This new career was a struggle, and in my insecurity I became obsessed with the idea that if I could only get married again that would solve everything.

The more frantic I was the worse my health became, yet the old fighting spirit would not give in. One day a friend said to me, "You should relax more—stop running around so much and be still. Why don't you come to church with me?"

I said "Okay" very condescendingly. You might have thought I was doing the church a favor! I heard a preacher who seemed to make sense, for the first time in my life. Then another friend suggested a church where I would meet "all sorts of nice people," and, still secretly hoping to find someone to marry, I joined this fashionable church.

It was a comfortable, elegant church and I liked it. Perhaps I was beginning to be a seeker after faith.

One day I saw a sign on a little church announcing that Gladys

Aylward, the famous missionary to China, would be speaking there. Having seen the film, "The Inn of the Sixth Happiness," suggested by her life story, I was eager to hear Miss Aylward. Here was a woman who had devoted her whole life to loving God and to serving people, and if she had asked me to go to Formosa with her I would have gone. She had *something,* and it was something I wanted very much.

I rushed to the next church where she was speaking, and again listened to her amazing story. Tears streamed down my face as I thought of all the orphans this little woman had cared for, was still caring for. I thought, *If I could only do a thing like that— something worthwhile—then my life would count for something.* When I met Miss Aylward, she said, "I can see you're seeking, and if you are you can't do better than to come here to Calvary Baptist Church."

I took her advice, and during the weeks that followed a new thought began to tug at my mind: *I needed saving.* This was strange, for I was accustomed to thinking of myself as quite a nice person, and took great pride in being independent.

Suddenly it dawned on me although I believed in Christ I had never received Him. How did one do this?

It was a simple little story that finally showed me what I was looking for. At a Sunday night service, our pastor used this illustration: "If you wanted to go to Brooklyn and I told you there was a bus right outside clearly marked, 'To Brooklyn,' and you saw the bus and asked the driver if it were the right one, and he told you, 'Yes, this is the way to Brooklyn,' and if you believed him—*but didn't get on the bus*—you'd *not* get to your destination."

Why that struck me I don't know, but I said to myself, "Joan, that's what's wrong. You're just missing the bus." The way to get where I wanted to go was to ask Christ to take me there.

At the end of the service there was an invitation to come forward to the front of the church if we wanted to trust God to
take over our lives. I made that decision, went forward to the
front, and then stayed on afterward for a meeting with the pastor.
What became clear to me in those moments was this: by the
simple act of sincerely asking Christ to come into our lives, we
do become children of God. It is an accomplished fact, and
nothing can change it.

I want to stress that I believe this step, though important, is
only the first. That very night I discovered just how much of an
"infant" I was, and how much there was to learn. When I got
home I knelt down by my dressing table, and that is when I had
what might be called the real "encounter" with the living God.

Suddenly I began to see myself as I must appear to Him.
How self-centered I was! What I felt for others was not compassion, but pity. I was pleasant to people only if I thought they
could be useful to me. I wanted to be liked, but inside I was
critical, impatient, and unloving.

It was a devastating revelation of my true character. I thought
back over my life and began to make confession of every shabby
thing I could remember. Trembling and weeping, I felt an awful
sense of repugnance for myself. I wanted to crawl into a corner
and die.

But then Christ seemed to be saying to me, in His wonderful
way, "This is all over—all forgiven. This is the end of the old
and the beginning of the new. This is *life,* Joan, and we're
starting fresh together."

The next morning I felt like a little girl on her birthday. I
wanted to laugh and shout to the whole world, "I've been born
again! I'm a child of God! I'm actually a child of God! Can you
believe it?" People I met that day said, "You look wonderful.
What happened?"

There was no question that my life was changed, and soon I saw just how drastically. To begin with, the terrible fear of illness—what would happen to me, all alone, if I should become sick again?—began to disappear. In a short while I realized whenever worry struck I could turn to the Lord, for He had promised to take care of me. Did I trust Him or not? It was that simple, but it was revolutionary.

The same thing was true of my career. Instead of going to an interview or an audition in fear and trembling, wondering frantically whether I'd get the job, now I found I was trusting God to control this, too.

Another important aspect of this new life was that I began to wonder if there were people I had hurt, anything I had done wrong which God wanted me to set right. Much was beyond recall, but there were acts of restitution I could make.

I remembered a young man I had worked for whom I had hurt very much. He was a Jew, and in his hearing I had carelessly used a common epithet for Jewish people—a word which clung to my vocabulary from my old life. I knew I must apologize, and though I shrank from it I simply set a time, promised the Lord I would do it, and then went ahead.

When the young man came out of his office to meet me, I said, "I've come to apologize. I need your forgiveness, Bob."

"Oh, now, Joan," he began, but I assured him it was important to me. "I should never have used that beastly word, and I shall never use it again. It was wrong of me, displeasing to God, and it hurt you. I'm terribly sorry."

Well, he put his arms around me and I kissed him. Of course, I explained what had happened to me, and told him of the change I felt. Then another extraordinary thing happened: this man, who had sworn never to hire me again, told me of a job opening on a television show.

Another matter of restitution was more diffcult. For years I had been helping English friends by keeping sums of money for them, in dollars, in my bank account. This was a convenience for them while they were in the States, but the bank account had become a crutch for me. I thought of it as a personal nest egg. In a pinch I could write to my friends and say, "Do you mind if I use some of your money?"

It wasn't honest, so I had to contact those people and explain the situation, and ask them to take their money off my hands because it had become a spiritual problem to me. I could not trust God fully while putting my trust in money—and money that wasn't even mine!

At another point my faith had a real test when a friend asked if she could borrow two hundred fifty dollars. That was all I had, and I too had bills coming due. My friend's situation, however, was desperate. I tried to get out of it as I prayed for advice, but God made it clear that He wanted me to help her. I swallowed hard, gave her the money, and determined to trust God for my own needs. He met those needs in a wonderful way, reaffirming what I was learning: that He is completely reliable and always keeps His word.

Having been independent and fending for myself for so many years, I find my greatest struggle is learning to let God do the work in and through me. I tend to do it alone, in my own strength, and I know this is always a mistake.

It's a curious and wonderful thing, this fact of being free: not having to depend on others, nor on myself. What I felt that momentous night, that it was the end of Joan and the beginning of *Christ in Joan,* has never left me. Through all the events, tests, failures, trials, victories, new growth, enlarging vision of the succeeding years, that great happiness is still with me. I have a long, long way to go, but accompanying this realization is the sense that God has a plan for me. Just think of it! My life, my future are His—and I ask you, could they be in better hands?

—January, 1961

Wherever she goes, Joan Gibbons creates a sensation. She has physical beauty and a "presence" which combines old-world elegance with today's chic. All of this becomes secondary when she speaks, however, for it is her Lord who dominates her conversation and her life. It was very soon after her conversion experience that Joan and I became friends. Because of her magnetism and the many attentions showered on her, I wondered whether she would become a "showpiece" for Christianity—a "nine days' wonder." I needn't have worried. Along with her new life, Joan was given the insight that in all things it is God, not she, who is to be glorified. Now at home in England, she continues to have a personal ministry and a vital share in planning for evangelism on a wider scale.

Chapter 6

■

MY FRIEND BOB

by Walden Howard
Editor, *Faith at Work* Magazine

I met him in a midtown Manhattan office—a plain, unimpressive room that comes alive once a week when ten or a dozen businessmen meet to share their spiritual ups and downs and to pray for one another before going back to work.

Each of us brings bits of his world to that office and shares them with the group. Before long all the experiences of life—its hopes and happiness and heartbreak—seem to unfold to form a mosaic in which each of us has a part.

From the first time Bob Arnold came to the group, he began to give us glimpses into his world, a world very different from our own. He told how his new life of surrender to God began, of his inner struggle to get more into the flow of life, and of the exciting way God was involving him with other people and speaking through him.

Why does God seem to use him more than most of us? Is it because he's a recent convert and hasn't yet gotten over the marvel of it? Or is it that as an artist he is more sensitive to the heart-cries of those about him?

His own explanation is that God uses him in spite of himself, that when he is filled with love he finds himself saying the right things and when people are helped he knows that God is doing it.

On that day in March when I first met him, he told us how it all began. Two weeks before, he had committed his life to Jesus Christ after a lifelong search for completeness.

Awhile back, Bob put his studio apartment on 58th Street up for lease. A painter, he had moved back into New York from Connecticut when his marriage broke up. The divorce had separated him from one he deeply loved. It triggered a deep distrust in himself. Was there something wrong with him? Was he incapable of mature love?

He wanted to know more of himself. Three sessions a week with a psychiatrist for a year helped to reassure him. But it did not displace the loneliness or end his search.

He was not painting. The inner well of inspiration had gone dry. Occasionally he would pause in a church to pray, but more often he relied on tranquilizers and martinis to keep him going. Then bill collectors began to pressure him and he put his apartment up for rent.

Joan Gibbons, along with many others, came to see the apartment and Bob showed her around. "You'll like it," he assured her. "It's very quiet. The only noise is on Sundays." He pointed to the back wall. "Through there is the organ of a church. You can hear it on Sunday mornings."

"Oh, that's my church," Joan smiled, "Calvary Baptist. Why don't you visit it some time?"

Attend a church service? Bob couldn't have cared less. At fourteen, in Delaware, he had joined a church. It was the thing to do. Over the years he had listened to an occasional radio preacher, and he had visited churches to admire their art. He had even painted his conception of Christ for a Presbyterian church on Long Island, but he had long ago stopped attending services. One would scarcely expect to find God in a church service!

Joan persisted. The fact that she is a lovely fashion model didn't hurt her cause, and finally Bob went. The people were "nice," and there was coffee after the service.

One day two years later, Joan called to tell of something special coming to her church. People from all over the world would be telling their own stories. The theme, "Under New Management," intrigued Bob. He went and sat with Joan through the opening meeting, and was intrigued even more by some of the stories.

Then they were assigned to small talk-it-over groups, according to the numbers on their name tags. When Bob sensed that he was to go one direction and Joan another, he panicked: "Don't leave me with these people." So she steered him to her own group which Sherry Day was leading.

When they introduced themselves around the circle, Bob said, quite honestly, "I'm searching." Sherry picked it up at once and when the meeting broke up his hand was on Bob's arm. "So you're searching. That's wonderful. Let's have a chat." The chat lasted two hours and Sherry's words made sense. The God who made the universe surely could manage Bob's life. But surrender to Him? Surrender his freedom?

The next night in his studio, Bob decided to try. He got on his knees and prayed but nothing seemed to happen. So on Sunday he went in search of Sherry. The conference was just breaking up and Sherry was running to catch a plane. But plans are made to be changed, and instead, Sherry sat down for the talk that led to Bob's surrender—the watershed of his life. Ever since, his conversation has been sprinkled with references to "before" and "after."

Bob walked on a cloud for weeks after that. It was like a honeymoon, the first enraptured days of a new relationship. He even caught himself singing out loud one day walking through

gloomy, cavernous old Pennsylvania Station. *Why am I singing?*
he wondered. *I haven't sung in years.*

He told us about that the same day he asked, "How do you
talk to a Jewish person?" Then the story came out. He had called
a friend and the friend's wife had answered.

"You sound tired, Cynthia."

"And why not? My mother is dying of cancer and I've been
spending every afternoon with her at the hospital. I'm ex-
hausted."

"Have you been going to your house of worship?"

"No, why?"

"Well, when you pour water out of a pitcher, as you've been
doing every day, you have to go somewhere to fill it up again."

"We've known you for years, Bob. We know you're not
religious. So what you say makes good sense."

When Bob told Sherry Day the story, Sherry chuckled, "Of
course you're not religious; you're alive!" Months later Bob had
his chance to tell Cynthia and her husband where his words had
come from.

One Tuesday Bob was beaming. He had talked the day before
to a taxi driver. Late for an appointment with an art director,
he hailed a cab. The driver started the conversation by saying,
"I'm glad you're going downtown because I've got to borrow
some money down there and then I'm going to the racetrack. . . . I know it's wrong. . . . I haven't been there for a
year. When I drive someone there, I put on blinders so I can't
see it. . . . I'm crazy to gamble. I have a wife and two kids. . . . I
need help!"

"You're like an alcoholic; aren't you?"

"Yeah."

By now they had pulled up to the curb. Bob said, "We all
go through some kind of hell." He told the driver about his

own, and about his commitment and the fellowship group, and then asked him about his faith.

"I'm Jewish."

"Well, we all pray to the same God. May I pray for you?"

"Yes."

"Right now, here?"

"Yes. . . . I think I'd like that."

He put his hand on the driver's arm and asked God to be with his new friend. As he opened his eyes, the driver smiled, "Gee, I feel better already."

One day Bob told us what happened Thanksgiving Eve on a train to Delaware. He was talking with a young husband when a chic little lady in her forties came up and Bob included her with, 'Hello, we're talking about children."

"Aren't they wonderful?" she responded. "I'm a nurse."

Abruptly she began to tell him her deep troubles. They talked for ten minutes or so and suddenly Bob realized her hands were in his. "Why don't you turn your problems over to the Lord?" he asked.

"I don't know how. When I was a little girl I was confirmed at church. I remember I had a big white ribbon in my hair. But nothing happened."

"Look," Bob said, "God has asked us to hand all our anxieties over to Him. I've done this, but sometimes I take them back and have to do it over again. You can do it."

He told her of God's power in creating all things, the beautiful design of the atoms, the negative and positive protons, the matter in the door handle of the railroad car, of all that we see and do not see.

She nodded, "It isn't what you've said so much as the way you've said it that's helped me. It is as though you spoke from your very soul."

"You're going to be all right now, aren't you?"

"Yes, I'll be all right." The train stopped. They said goodbye. She was gone.

The matter that Bob brings most often to the group has gotten him so involved that soon he will go to court against New York's largest newspaper to try to end an injustice in his neighborhood.

He moved last year, during the newspaper strike, into his present apartment. It was a quiet, peaceful neighborhood. Then the strike was settled. And suddenly he found himself living in bedlam.

His apartment house is across from the warehouse of the newspaper where from eight at night to six in the morning the high-pitched whine of the hoist that unloads the 1,800-pound rolls of newsprint, together with the banging and shouting of the indifferent workers, makes conversation and sleep virtually impossible.

A dozen families in the apartment house have suffered this abuse for over two years and failed to get it stopped by appeals to the newspaper, the mayor's department, and police. No one would touch the problem.

Bob's first thought was to break his lease and move. After all, the apartment had been rented to him under false pretenses. But as he talked to some others in the building, and sensed their frustration and helplessness, he decided that he couldn't move.

God gave him the conviction that he should stay and fight, not for himself, but for those who had no alternative but to live under these intolerable conditions.

He has organized the residents, hired a lawyer, and is bringing suit against a newspaper that has laughed off previous complaints and seemingly feels secure in its ability to break the law and disregard the rights of its neighbors.

One of the people Bob has helped is a member of our group.

When John came to town last fall, he was referred to us by a Christian girl he had dated at the University of Colorado, who was "different." He soon discovered that Bob, too—along with the others of us—had what made the difference.

One night he showed up at Bob's apartment. Over the noise of whining hoists he and Bob talked for an hour or two. As he was leaving, John said, "I believe, but . . .

"What is this *but*?" Bob asked.

"The Lord hasn't spoken to me."

"Look here. I don't know much about this, but I don't think God is going to come right out and speak to you. Let's pray."

As John started down the steps, in his excitement he walked past the elevator. Bob called him back.

John laughed, "Isn't it wonderful? It's fantastic! All I needed was fellowship."

Then it was time for Bob to share the excitement, for he sensed once again, as John did, that Someone Else was there with them. "Now what more do you want God to do?" Bob asked in obvious delight. "You asked Him to fill you and He did."

Every Tuesday, almost, brings such a story. We listen and thank God. What a different man Bob is today than when I met him one year ago. He still has a long way to go. He's the first to admit that. But God is using him, and we're all different for his sharing his life with us.   *—March, 1964*

As this is written, Bob Arnold is in Vietnam. He has been there for many months, working with the USO. It has not been an easy job. He has suffered frustration, discouragement, and serious physical illness—not to mention the exhaustion that comes from working nearly around the clock seven days a week. But he intends to stay on until he has yet another USO unit in operation. I mention this not to flatter Bob—he wouldn't like that—but to indicate how thoroughgoing and far-reaching is the change in his life. How many of us can imagine leaving an interesting and rather "soft" life in the United States to traipse halfway around the word to tackle such a thankless task? This selflessness is an authenticating mark of the new life in Christ which Bob Arnold exemplifies. Wherever he goes, he ministers.

Chapter 7

∎

DISCOVERY

by Bernard B. Gair
Public School Teacher (retired), Brooklyn, New York

It was in the early years of the Great Depression that I first faced the challenge of Jesus Christ. Quite by accident I met some people who by word and manner showed that they had "something." That something was a quality of life with a serenity and a sense of purpose that was quite foreign to my experience.

By contrast my own life seemed shabby, inhibited, and shallow, and I became aware of pretense and inadequacy. I left that first group with a hunger for the kind of assurance and inner freedom I saw there.

Outwardly, I was as conventionally happy and well-adjusted as the next man. Accounted to be reasonably successful in my work as a teacher, I got on pretty well with people. But inwardly I was restless and dissatisfied. I suffered much from self-consciousness and an anguished sense of inadequacy about life in general. More than anything I wanted people to like me, and to praise me, especially for my "intellectual" qualities. A philosophical temperament was offset by a strong ambition to rise in the economic scale—to make good.

I succeeded admirably in keeping my associates from knowing the kind of person I was on the inside. One can establish a

55

"front" if he works at it, and I conveyed to all who knew me a front of self-sufficiency. At least I *thought* so!

My personal philosophy was an idealistic one, and had an almost idolatrous faith in the perfectibility of society through the avenues of education and social reform. Humanism was my religion. It never dawned on me that an unrealistic gap existed between my social outlook and my personal conflicts.

I had rarely given any serious thought to being "in step with God." "Salvation" seemed a pious abstraction, unrelated to being "a success" or improving society. If I thought at all of a condition for "being saved," I supposed that decent behavior and generally honest intentions would be it.

As a Jew, I had received the traditional instruction in parts of the Old Testament and certain Talmudic commentaries. In common with all Jewish children of my acquaintance I was required to attend religious classes after school hours and on Sundays, up to the age of thirteen. That is the age of Bar Mitzvah, when Jewish boys are officially and ceremoniously admitted into full membership in the Community of Israel.

By that age, I had been duly indoctrinated by our rabbi into the basic concepts of our religion: God is One; God loves righteousness above all; and God chose a people, Israel, to share with the world His ideals of purity and goodness and justice. My brothers and I learned to recite conventional prayers, and to use the phylacteries, which are injoined upon devout Jews (Deuteronomy 6:8, 11:18). Obediently I accompanied my father to Sabbath services every Friday evening and Saturday morning and on holy days. I am certain that the seeds of love for God were sown during these early years, and I am very grateful for them.

With the years I acquired a growing appreciation for Jesus as a great moral teacher in the sacred tradition of rabbis like Hillel, and prophets like Hosea and Isaiah. He fitted in with my own pattern of idealistic thinking. I often thought of Him as a social revolutionary, whose teachings, if followed, would transform our social order and bring in an era of peace and plenty for all. In the furthest outreach of imagination however, I was not prepared to see Jesus as the Messiah, God-made-man for our salvation.

My newly acquired friends put no pressure on me to accept any dogma about Jesus. They simply held Him up as "the way," and invited me to travel in it. A person could learn a lot about himself, they showed, by measuring himself against the straight edges of the moral law, summarized by Jesus' principles. One could begin to see more clearly the imperfections, the dishonesties in his own life.

So a new word came alive in my vocabulary: *sin*. It was not a word held in repute in educated circles, or considered in good taste. People made mistakes, had faults, failed to achieve, suffered from complexes, but—sins? No.

Yet there it was, truly descriptive of the rebellious nature of men like myself, men living for themselves and knowing no higher authority than their own desires, or interests, or ambitions.

I thank God for the realism and definiteness of these Christians. Was I willing to make an honest assessment of my life, as measured by God's standards as seen in Jesus? After such an inventory, revealing "me" to myself and showing me the blocks separating me from God, would I be willing to offer up the burden of my failures to God and seek His forgiveness?

Further, was I willing to yield to Him the governance of my life, and live henceforth according to His will and by the power of His Spirit? That would mean a compact with God. I would abdicate sovereignty of myself and my affairs, and He would daily guide me, strengthen me, teach me, and feed me from a new center.

And finally how was I to *know* for certain that I was building on spiritual bedrock, and not on escapism or wish-fulfillment?

As I wrestled with these matters I came to see that Christian faith need not negate the teachings of Moses and the Hebrew prophets, with their inflexible straight edge of law. That had been a schoolmaster, a training ground for the spirit, a revelation of man's need for a Redeemer.

Had He come? Jesus had identified Himself with our all-too-human nature. By His death had He brought about the atonement for our sins? I began to see that Jesus was indeed He who had been previsioned by the Old Testament sages and recorded in holy accents in their Scriptures, the spotless lamb of the temple. The Lamb of God—the Messiah—the Saviour—the Son of God.

Philosophers and theologians talk much about conversion. They analyze its component, psychological parts; they describe the prerequisite conditions leading up to it. But when it happens, and God begins to move within a person, he *knows* and further discussion becomes academic.

I heard many Christians testify to the change in themselves, and I was hungry to know for myself. What I describe above did not happen quickly. I read the Bible with my heart as well as with my mind. I prayed and talked with experienced Christians about the areas in my life that were only known to God and myself. Then one day I was moved to make a decision. *It happened!* With this I experienced a tremendous release and something new came to birth in me.

A good many years have now passed since that first decision. I encountered much ridicule and resistance as I tried to live out my faith. I knew the pain of failure, as old habits and weaknesses reasserted themselves while the new faith was "digging in." I had to learn about the resources which God provides for the struggle. Spiritual discipline did not come easy to one who had lived without the presence and grace of God for almost four decades. But I had drunk of a fountain of living water, and I kept coming back.

One special discipline cried for an answer: How was I to find time for consistent prayer and communion with God? For me it worked out best to arise earlier, even an hour before the usual time. There in this time of quiet prayer and meditation I soon learned to face myself again and bring the demands of the day before the Lord, and accept His forgiveness and cleansing and wise counsel. A new clarity and previously unknown charity began to flood my mind and heart; a new dimension of experience was opened.

Further, I saw that the Christian life was not a solitary thing, "the flight of the alone to the Alone." I had to seek fellowship and an opportunity to help others and be helped in spiritual growing-up.

As I now seek God's mind, daily bringing to Him my stubbornness of heart and the failures of temper and pride, I come to know both the beauty and the power of forgiveness and the liberation of the ever "new start." As I see what the Church offers—the services, the sacraments, the fellowship—the personal companionship of Jesus has become the most precious thing in my life. It is a shared companionship with a common witness to the love and grace of God revealed in His Son. Here is the family in which Jew and Gentile are one; and each having the joy of being Christ's ambassador.

As a teacher, my primary concern is to prepare students to live in a real world, to face real problems, and to help build up the requisite skills and attitudes to deal with life. I find myself compelled to call attention to the glaring fact of conflict—conflict in the lives of people, and among classes, groups, and nations. But it is also my duty now to help interpret the conflicts, indicate their causes and backgrounds, and, even more important, to indicate in what direction solutions may be sought.

—*December, 1953*

Listening to Bernie Gair talk about the Bible is an unforgettable experience. He draws on the deathless Hebrew heritage which is naturally his, and makes the ancient signs, stories, and symbols come glowingly alive. Christ as Messiah has never seemed more real to me than in Bernie's life and witness. Recently retired as a public school teacher, he has profoundly affected the lives of many youngsters over the years—never through coercion, but through the combination of a brilliant mind, a warm heart, exemplary scholarship, and deep faith.

Chapter 8

■

IS THIS REALLY ME?

by Audrey M. Lundy
Government Official, Newmarket, Ontario

Am I the same person as the bundle of misery that walked
this earth six months ago? I can hardly believe it.

I was a split personality. One person in me was a good churchgoing, Sunday-school-teaching perfectionist. The other was an
unhappy, dejected, guilt-ridden, hateful, resentful being.

I was "saved" as a child. At twenty-one I made a public confession of Christ in a Baptist church in Toronto, but He never
became real to me. He was off in the clouds, viewing me with
reproach and condemnation. I was filled with hatred and in-
feriority and inhibitions.

This went on for years until I was terrified at what was happening to me. It's a wonder to me now that I didn't murder
somebody in the black hatred that filled my heart.

With many misgivings I arrived at a Christian Ashram in
Belleville, Ontario, late in June. I had wavered about coming,
and as soon as I arrived I knew I didn't fit in. I felt unwanted
and rejected. Everyone seemed happy and I was miserable.

I landed in a prayer group that was led by a very beautiful
young woman and I hated her for being beautiful. I had been
told that one person could block the Holy Spirit in a group, and

61

I thought, *I'll fix her pretty little clock; I'll spoil this prayer group.* And I did.

Only after the battle had been won did we become friends. Then she confided to me that I not only spoiled the group, but that she knew I had set out to do it.

As the internal battle raged, I finally ran up to my room, threw my name tag at the dresser, and said out loud, "I hate everybody here and everybody hates me. I'm going home." I jammed my clothes angrily into my suitcase and called the bus station to ask when the next bus left.

I was told that there wasn't another bus until two o'clock the next morning. (I think it was a mistake, and I think God ordained it.) So I sat sullenly in my room until hunger pangs overcame me. At six o'clock I thought, *To heck with these people. I paid my money and I'll go and get some supper.*

I sat down at a table. A lady came toward me, turned away, paused, and came back. She told me later that the Holy Spirit prompted her to return. And in that simple act God, who flung the stars in their place, showed that he was personal enough to care for a person like me, and put beside me a wonderful, loving Christian.

When I asked for a second cup of tea, she saw the pot was empty and went to another table to get some. Only then did I notice that she was terribly lame. That rocked me. Here was someone who was willing to go the second mile for me when every step was painful.

Going out of the dining room, she linked her arm in mine, and as I turned to thank her for her kindness an electric shock went through me. I saw the love of Christ in her eyes as I had never seen it before. Everything in me leaped out to Him—I wanted Him. Through my mind went the thought, *There's an answer to my need here somewhere.*

As we talked my new friend said, "God wants you." Then she began to pray and as she did the Lord came so close I could almost touch Him. He wasn't looking at me in anger. His eyes were full of love and sorrow and hurt. Oh, how I loved Him.

I went back to my room, unpacked, put my name tag back on, and stayed at the Ashram.

Before long God showed me something I had to do. Bruce Larson was preaching on the last day. When he finished he sat down in the audience. I have always been self-conscious, but now I didn't care what anyone thought. I went over to Bruce and said, "Please help me."

We slipped out to a quiet room and I shared the past with him, with all its guilt and shame and unhappiness and failure. Bruce listened and then said, "Now we're going to get splinters in our knees." We got down and gave it all to Christ. And at that moment He set me free.

Every area of life has changed in the weeks that have followed. No longer do I lie in bed in the morning, dreading to start the day. No longer do I fear encounters with other people. Even my appearance is changing. I'm standing up straight and erect. (After all, I'm a child of God.) At church last Sunday I went over to speak to a man I have known all my life, and he didn't recognize me.

One of the first things I did when God released me was to ask Him to use me "to bind up the broken-hearted and set the prisoner free." I can identify with both. And He has been doing just that.

One day a friend said to me, "Audrey, you seem so different." There was my chance to tell her about Christ. Soon after she called to ask if we could talk again. We did and she took her problems to Christ.

The post office has been busy, too. A friend in Sweden heard of my father's death and wrote to express sympathy. I wrote back of my experience and she replied at once, telling me her problems. The letters have been flying like sixty. I heard from her the other day and she was vibrating with happiness. "Audrey," she wrote, "what else can I do but surrender to Christ?"

I have recently had another letter from my friend in Sweden in which she tells of rejoicing in Christ, and that He is blessing and undertaking in her home.

Shortly after Christ became real and vital to me, a friend called asking me to have lunch with her. During the meal she poured out her problems, then asked me about mine. I replied, "I have none." She countered, "Oh, you must have; everybody has problems." I replied again that I had none. When she asked, "How come?" I told her that I found that Christ is the answer to all our problems, and that He can undertake in a remarkable way when we surrender everything to Him. We went to the car and talked some more, and before we parted my friend placed herself and all her problems into the hands of our loving Lord.

Now Christ, by His Spirit, has entered into every department of my life, for I have surrendered it all, totally and unreservedly. I am a whole person at last—outgoing, at ease, and radiantly happy.

                                                    —*December, 1963*

Audrey Lundy's story appeared in FAITH AT WORK while I was not on the magazine staff, so I read it from the point of view of any casual subscriber. What struck me at once was the intense practicality of her conversion experience: this was no fantasy, no "pie in the sky" fairy tale, but the down-to-earth account of a rather disagreeable person who underwent a transformation which altered her attitudes, her behavior, even her appearance, in ways which were immediately apparent. What is more, Miss Lundy has never reneged on the new steps she took in 1963. She found out who she really was, and it "took."

Chapter 9

■

RELUCTANT DISCIPLE

by Victor Strom
Manager, Port Authority Building, New York City

The morning sun's bright rays burst through the stained glass windows like a rainbow, helping to dispel my slight feeling of uneasiness. I settled back in the church pew as the service progressed, but my mind wandered that morning in the autumn of 1956. I started to think about the hundreds of other Sundays I had spent in that church, surrounded by family and friends.

Except for two periods of service with the Navy during World War II and the Korean War, I had been a faithful churchgoer all my life. Here I had been baptized. Here I had attended Sunday school and confirmation classes under the guidance of devoted laymen and pastors. Here, during adolescence, I had "graduated" to the eleven o'clock service with the grownups.

Frequently I approached Sunday mornings with the vague hope that something meaningful would happen. Many times I went away with an inner glow, warmed and touched by some aspect of the service. But by Monday morning the glow had faded, and I was again confronted with the conflicts and problems of business and social life.

I had recently been appointed Assistant Manager of the Port Authority Building, sharing responsibility for the operation and maintenance of a fifteen-story, block-long, block-wide complex

of office and warehouse space housing the home offices of the
Port of New York Authority. Outwardly confident, I was inwardly afraid that I might not prove equal to this job. There
were 170 men and women involved in this operation, and every
one of their problems, insofar as it affected their work, became
a problem of mine.

At the same time my social life was becoming a bitter disappointment—an endless round of parties and one brief romance
after another. These relationships always disintegrated, and I
can see how much of an "island" I was, not wanting to give too
much of myself for fear of being hurt or made the fool. I began
to wonder if I would ever be happily married.

Then I met Neva, a vivacious brunette whose easy, outgoing
nature immediately put me at ease. First dates are usually reserved for fact-finding, and ours was no different, except that by
the end of the evening we were discussing things I had never
spoken of with another girl, even superficially. Neva talked
frankly about her own life, telling of a broken home, a period
of insecurity at a boarding school, a long search to find herself,
and then of her contact with the lively young adult group at a
downtown church. She outlined the influence of the vital Christians she had met, and how she had come to commit her life to
Christ.

Never had a girl revealed her innermost thoughts to me so
openly and unashamedly. I could not question or make light of
what she said.

Soon after this meeting, my superior became ill and I was
appointed Acting Manager of the Port Authority Building.
Knowing that all my decisions and actions were being scrutinized,
I constantly fought my own doubts as to my ability to cope with
the job.

Meanwhile, I saw Neva more and more often. I started to go

to church with her, and there I met responsible young people who not only seemed to accomplish a lot, but who reflected an attitude and a vigor that impressed me. There was a fellowship group, a hard core of men and women in the young adults organization, which consisted primarily of people who had taken Christ on as a partner in their daily activities. I was intrigued, but my stubborn Norwegian reserve kept me from going too far into this unknown territory.

When Neva and I became engaged, we knelt together—at her suggestion—and prayed aloud. This was probably my first positive step at this stage of spiritual development. Though she often spoke of the fellowship group, she never urged me to participate. For years I had adopted a secretive, defensive attitude about my religion, telling myself that it was a very personal thing and that where I stood with God was no one's business but His and mine. This attitude protected me from those who might have exposed the fact that my faith was a hollow shell coated with a veneer of churchgoing, automatic prayers, and a nice moral front that could be dropped easily.

A few weeks after we became engaged, I received a permanent appointment as Manager of the Building. At first elated, I soon began to feel the added weight of responsibility, especially in view of the fact that I would soon be married.

The following February I went with Neva and a group of friends from the young adults on a retreat weekend. There I listened as people told of the part Christ played in their lives. I heard of difficulties that had seemed impossible to cope with until God's love and power were accepted. It was the first time I had heard people speak of the Saviour as a down-to-earth, positive force. I was impressed—but not sold! Still, before the weekend was over, I was moved to tell a bit of my own past spiritual growth—or lack of it—and to say that I felt impelled to commit to God my approaching marriage. I returned home refreshed, but soon found the rosy glow fading.

After our marriage in April, 1958, Neva and I faced the same crises, both trivial and major, that newlyweds have faced since the days of Adam and Eve. My commitment to God of our marriage, unsupported by anything other than a moment of resolve, faded into nothing. Adjustment to the "double harness" did not come easily.

But in June we attended another weekend retreat, and again I felt challenged to positive action. For the first time I admitted to another individual that all was not well with Vic Strom. "Where do I go from here?" I asked.

The friend I had sought out countered with the story of his own conversion, and suggested we pray together. In the midnight quiet we bowed our heads and prayed aloud. Although the setting and the mood were perfect, something kept me from taking the step of a personal commitment to God, and I left that weekend deeply troubled.

With autumn came a twist of fate that transferred me from one Naval Reserve unit to another, with a different meeting night. Now I had no valid reason for not attending fellowship meetings, and I began to go regularly with Neva. Each time brought a new, more meaningful experience. On several occasions we went directly from a frustrating disagreement at home to a discussion which precisely hit on the source of our trouble. At such times we went away feeling that God had touched us.

Apparently some people at the church thought I had progressed more than I actually had. A Holy Thursday program was being planned, and I was asked to be one of a group of men to portray the Disciples at the Last Supper. Moreover, we were to speak to the group out of our own experiences and convictions. Not knowing how to refuse graciously, I accepted this assignment.

Then began two troubled weeks. What would I say? What *could* I say? I couldn't get up in front of the group and pretend to be something I was not. It would be especially incongruous while representing one of the Disciples—almost sacrilegious.

Holy Thursday arrived, and still I had made no decision. As night approached and my co-workers left, I closed the door of my office and pondered the dilemma. Staring out into the twilight, I asked myself why I was holding back from making a complete commitment of my life to Christ. Immediately the answer came that I was afraid. Suddenly I remembered that years before I had come to this very point, but gone no further for fear of having to give up some of the world's pleasures that seemed so important to me.

Now I thought about the people I had come to know who had surrendered themselves to God. They hadn't been "deprived" —in fact, they were enjoying the kind of riches that can't be bought! I saw that in my happy marriage and interesting work I had all that the world could give. Anything beyond this could come only from God Himself.

So right there at my desk I prayed, "Dear Lord, I commit my whole being to Thee, now and forever more. Use me as you see fit."

Probably there was no visible change in me, but there was certainly a change within. I was turned from a man who looked to God only in times of trouble or need to one with an absolute certainty of the constant presence of Christ. If there are still days when God seems far away, I nevertheless find my faith growing and my lapses fewer as time passes.

From time to time my ego rears its head, and I'm tempted to take back those areas in my life which have been given to God, but I'm also learning how to pray for an open mind so that His will is done.

Life is still hectic, but my anxiety is gone. Prayer frees me from worry and fear in making decisions. Things have changed on the job, too. I have tried to take a personal interest in the men who work for me. With some of my co-workers I have shared my experience, and this has brought a closeness and understanding and a smoothness in our working together that were absent before.

Also, I find that I have a great desire to express my faith to others. This isn't easy, but no one ever said being a Christian is an easy task! Christ is no sop for the weak or willy-nilly, but a source of strength and power for all who reach out and seek Him.

—*January, 1961*

If you could have another brother, Vic Strom is just the man you might choose. He has quiet, solid strength that makes the old term "true blue" meaningful again. Sometimes I have watched Vic interact with a group of men—both fellow Christians and seekers—and have marveled at the faith and generosity which lie beneath his calm exterior. It occurs to me that the first disciples may have been men like Vic: feet on the ground, heads in the clouds, capable of turning the world upside down. He and his wife Neva make a remarkable team: Neva sparkles, Victor glows.

Chapter 10

■

THE BIG SWITCH

by Margaret Austin
Housewife, Houston, Texas

This is the story of the big switch, from paganism to Christianity. As for personal background, I will make it short. I was born, baptized, confirmed, married, had two children, was divorced, and a few years ago I wound up in Houston working as a court reporter. I hadn't been to church in fourteen years.

The only thing I can say for myself at that point in my life is that I had become aware something was in the universe besides people. But the concept that there was a Being who was even remotely concerned with people was, I felt, presumptuous and unrealistic, and anyone who believed such a thing had holes in his head.

When the children and I came to Houston, I decided that as long as we were living in a so-called Christian country I should at least expose them to the church. So I shopped around for a church that wouldn't offend my pseudo-intellectual sensibilities. I went to a couple of different ones and thought they were nice—dull but nice.

Soon afterward, my little girl had a birthday. We didn't know any children to invite to a party. My older girl said she knew a nice girl at school, and when I looked up her father's name in the phone book I found a *reverend* in front of it. I thought, *Oh, no, a preacher's family.*

But because my little girl wanted a party so badly, I got my courage up and called them. It turned out there were four children in the family and they all came—plus the mother.

I was wary of her even though she sounded quite human over the phone. What a surprise to discover that she was good-looking and had a lot of zip. We had a nice afternoon and when she left I told her if her husband wanted to tangle with a good agnostic to send him over. I thought I was so smart I could confound him.

This preacher and his wife were Clax and Vicky Monro. Both had been agnostics at one time, so they knew what it was like to believe in not much of anything. They knew the questions about religion which plagued me—and the answers. They spoon-fed me with simple Christian truths and gently led me to St. Stephen's Episcopal Church.

The first service I attended was a most unhappy experience. I believed nothing of what I heard and could not, with honesty, read the prayers. I spent the hour mute, angry, and rebellious, wondering how these people could teach this unrealistic nonsense to children—much less expect grownups to swallow it.

When the service was over, I couldn't get out of the church fast enough. I was afraid someone I knew would see me and think I had flipped.

That afternoon Vicky called and told me about a service at the church that evening. Lay people were going to talk about what God had done in their lives. Did I want to go? Her invitation was relaxed. I felt free to go or not go. Had I ever felt I was being forced into the Church, I would have been over the hill and gone.

Initially my religion was founded on people and what I saw

in them. I went that evening because I liked Vicky and Clax. Later on I began to look to God, but at first I had to look to people because I didn't believe in God.

Clax started that night by saying that in his opinion the layman's ministry had been neglected, and from then on Sunday nights would be dedicated to laymen speaking on what their faith meant to them. As a start he was going to tell his own story, but from then on this service would belong to the laymen.

He told us about turning from agnosticism to the ministry. It was interesting to hear how an MIT graduate made the trip, but it didn't really get to me because the very fact that he *was* a minister made him different from "just people." What had happened to him might be valid, but it couldn't possibly happen to a person like me.

From then on I continued to attend church on Sunday mornings and evenings. I heard lawyers, writers, salesmen, and housewives. I did not really believe what they said, but I liked the people. There were qualities about them I had never seen before. They were utterly sincere, and reflected well-being, happiness. For years I had thought happiness was confined to the very young or idiots.

But here I heard laughter—wonderful, fullbodied laughter. There was a glow on the faces of these people, and I couldn't help but wonder where it came from. I found I wanted some of this glow for myself. The clincher was that I saw married people look at each other as if they liked each other. That was a shock.

The weight of the evidence was piling up. After three months I went to Clax and told him that I couldn't buy this Christianity but I wanted to try it anyway. What should I do? How does one who doesn't believe in God go about trying to live a God-centered life?

Bless his heart. He didn't talk about faith or trust or turning my life over to God. He just told me to experiment. He told me to act as though God existed and to see if it worked.

Also, he told me to read something of a spiritual nature every day. I thought to myself, *Boy, that is the dullest thing I ever heard of.* I did it anyway. He told me to pray. *Gimme this. Gimme that.* All my prayers were said flat on my back in bed.

Soon I realized that gimme prayers were children's prayers and if I was going to give this spiritual business a fair shake, I had to put some real effort into it.

It is a very difficult thing to put one's faith and trust in something he does not believe in. But it was necessary to do just that. I had to find out if God was true. I *had to* trust something I didn't believe in.

Feeling ridiculous, and knowing that it wouldn't possibly work, I proceeded on my first experiment.

It was a dilly. I purposely chose the most difficult problem in my life. This problem was hatred for a person which I had held for many years. It was a deep, fullblown hate and one which I felt was perfectly justified. My project was to get rid of this feeling.

This experiment was coupled with the first kneeling prayer I had said since I was a child. To get on my knees and bow my head was, in itself, a rough thing to do because I was proud and until that time had bowed my head to no one. The combination of kneeling prayer plus praying for this hated person was a sweat-provoking ordeal. I tried and tried to pray for this person, to wish him well. I failed. I just couldn't even whisk one tiny prayer through my head.

The next day I was triumphant in a nauseating sort of way because I felt that obviously God, if He worked at all, certainly didn't work in the area of taking away personal hatred.

Then I thought, *Well, maybe this isn't a one-shot deal; maybe I had better try again.* That night, with much agony of soul, I was able to slide one prayer through my bottled-up brain. That prayer consisted only of a very small wish for this person. I sent it through to a God I didn't believe in and asked Him to send it on. The whole procedure was as hard for me as to cut off my arm with a dull knife.

By the third night the whole thing had developed into a personal challenge. It was so difficult that I was curious to see if I could do it again. So once more I knelt down, and—wonder of wonders—articulated an almost presentable prayer for this hated person. At that moment God lifted the incredible burden off my shoulders and I went to bed and slept like a child.

From this experience I received a glimmer of the freedom in which a practicing Christian lives: freedom from guilt, hate, anxiety, and fear.

Then my so-called rational mind started sawing away, and it came up with the idea that psychologically this thing I had been doing was very sound. Think well of a person, and you can't hate him. So, unbeliever that I was, I set the whole experience down to good psychology.

At that time, having great belief in the strength of the human mind and no belief in God, I was not prepared to give God the credit.

So I tried another experiment. That one I called "Peace in the Home." I would like to present myself as a nicer person than I was, but it is necessary to say that as a pagan I was utterly selfish, domineering with the children, and with no ability to love anyone.

It is important to understand that I was not aware of these qualities, or lack of them. I thought I was just fine; "peachy-keen," in fact: clever, smart, and really quite a girl. But my insides didn't match the outside. God gave me the insight to know that I wasn't what I ought to be, but that all was not lost. With His help I could become a nicer person.

So I prayed for peace in the home, for me to be more loving, more kind, more just. I prayed to remember that the girls were God's children as well as mine. At first the change in the house was erratic and nebulous, but so were my prayers. Nevertheless, whenever I remembered to pray a good, honest prayer, the change of feeling in our home was immeasurable.

It took me a long time to realize that the change in the house was the result of prayer. At first I set it down to coincidence, but there is a point beyond which coincidence doesn't fit. It had to be God working in our lives. There was no other explanation.

But I had to try more. The third experiment was the clincher. Tithing time came up and the first idea that crossed my brain was, *Here's the hook. This is the reason they want me in church. They want a bigger head count and also my money.* But I thought I might as well shoot the works, so I tithed, saying to myself as I have said so many times since, "This is the most ridiculous thing I have ever done." I wanted to know whether God bothered with finances. I practically died when I filled out that tithing card. This was *my* money. I earned it and obviously with a big hunk of money going down the drain I wouldn't be able to meet all my bills. Something had to give.

As with everything else in this wonderful spiritual life, things didn't work out that way. Quite the contrary. Not only did I have enough to pay bills, but my wishes for material things subtly changed. In a strange way I didn't need the things I had thought I needed before. So my money went further. The greatest blessing to come from this was that I lost my fear of not having enough for our needs. I realized that if I did my part and worked hard, our needs would be met. Another strange thing happened in that I lost interest in money as such. It no longer became a golden dream of a never-never land where money and happiness were synonymous. I was finding happiness without money, and the tithing check became the one check it was fun to write.

Something else happened which made a great change in my life. I have always been one for living six months ahead when everything would be different. One day I drove into the driveway to the house and a new thought was born in me with great strength. The thought was, *Nothing has changed; same house, same job, same children, yet everything is different from the time I began trying to be a Christian.* In a wonderful way happiness and peace were part of my life where before there was discord, wishful thinking, and considerable unhappiness. I got out of the car and went to greet the girls thinking, *This is it, this is my life and by the grace of God I will learn to live within its limitations and to live a productive, happy, even joyful life.*

God Himself has taught me to look at life with no illusions and no sentimentality, and to accept it exactly as it is, but at the same time to enjoy it with a singing heart.   —*October, 1959*

I met Margaret Austin at a conference in the Pocono Mountains in 1959. She had come from Texas with several other lay people and with Claxton Monro, Rector of St. Stephen's Church in Houston, to describe that church's "witnessing fellowship," then in its early years. A tall, handsome woman with a marvelous speaking voice, she had a no-nonsense gift for getting at the heart of the matter in any discussion of authentic Christianity. Perhaps because of her experimental approach, and certainly because of her acute intelligence, she was able to separate the wheat from the chaff. These qualities are evident in her story, and help to make it one of my favorites of all the hundreds I have edited for FAITH AT WORK.

Chapter 11

■

GOD'S HAND
WAS ON MY SHOULDER

by Otto Schwarz
Post Office Superintendent, Newark, New Jersey

In January, 1941, at the age of seventeen, I joined the United States Navy, and after a short training period was swallowed up in a world fast heading toward the disaster of World War II.

My father was killed when I was ten and after that I began to drift away from the family—and at the same time to drift away from the church in which I'd been reared. Looking back, I have the impression of a religion which led me to fear the wrath of God, but didn't place much emphasis on His love, or the fact that He lives with us day by day. Leaving school in my sophomore year, I secured my mother's permission to join the Civilian Conservation Corps, which took me from Newark to California, and not long after that I was a sailor on my way to the Philippines.

On March 1, 1942, my ship, the heavy cruiser U.S.S. Houston, was sunk off the coast of Java, with a loss of almost eight hundred men. When the order came to abandon ship, I was at my battle station in the powder magazine, well below the water line. Leading a procession of fourteen men from one smoke-filled compartment to another, at one point I made a right turn. I felt the man behind me drop his hand from my shoulder and turn left. At that instant a torpedo hit nearby and all my companions perished. Only I made it to the upper deck.

When I got there another shell hit. The men around me and I were all thrown to the deck as hot shrapnel and burning debris filled the air. Seeing that my upper body was unprotected by clothing, one of my shipmates threw himself across my body, and again I narrowly escaped death. God had His hand on my shoulder, but I didn't know it.

All during the night the Japanese patrolled the dark waters, machine-gunning survivors. A boat approached me, and I thought certainly this was the end. I lowered my head in the water and hoped for the best. I could hear the Japanese chattering as they poked my body with a boat hook. Evidently thinking I was already dead, they pulled away.

After an eight-or-nine hour swim I was picked up by a landing barge and taken prisoner of war, along with 350 other survivors. This was the beginning of almost four years of indescribable torture, starvation, and illness.

We worked on the infamous Burma-Thai Railway, running through the Burma jungles from Rangoon to Bangkok. In eighteen months, about 116,000 lives were lost through disease, starvation, and mistreatment. Our captors seemed to have absolutely no regard for human life; even their own men, when they got out of line, were treated savagely.

Somehow I lived on. Don't ask me how. From time to time I'd pray, but it was a kind of automatic thing, and I never thought my prayers were really being answered. I credited everything to luck—good or bad. My motto was, "Whatever will be, will be."

There were times, to be sure, when I didn't want to live, when the physical hardship got to be too much. In retrospect I can understand that God still had His hand on my shoulder, though this was hardly a reality to me.

Finally, in 1945, we were released. I came home, got married, settled down. But for several years I was still filled with hatred for the Japanese. Gertrude, my wife, didn't dare bring anything to the house which had been made in Japan. Bit by bit this anger and resentment faded away, until it left me completely. Now I have no feelings of hatred at all for our World War II enemies. Their attitude toward life was contrary to everything we believe in, but I can't hate them for it any more.

As the years passed I was outwardly very happy. I had a wife, children, a home, a job—everything a man can ask from life. Having married a Presbyterian girl I found a new approach to religion. I soon joined the church and became involved in its activities. I was an usher, a Cub Scout master, president of the Board of Deacons, and a Sunday school teacher.

Nevertheless I walked around under a cloud of dissatisfaction. Each year my family life got a little worse. Certainly I wasn't an easy fellow to get along with. Gertrude and the kids never knew what to expect from me when I got home from work—I was always "blowing my top," and then my wife and I would be at each other's throats. This bothered me—and yet I was doing all the things I thought I should be doing.

Despite all my church activities I didn't feel "different." Sure, I closed my eyes and prayed hard when reciting the Apostles' Creed, and every time I partook of the Communion service I wanted Christ to enter my life. But nothing ever "happened."

Another thing—I started to see only the bad side of people's characters. Working closely with people gave me a chance to get a good look at human nature, and I didn't like it. My fellow church members especially came in for a lot of mental criticism. When I'd been just a worshipper, not paying attention to anyone, it was okay, but getting to know people intimately made me see only the evil in them and none of the good. I was rapidly turning into an "angry young man," and becoming more unhappy as time passed.

At times there seemed to be no possibility of reconciliation between my wife and me. We never really *talked* about anything. Gertrude dreaded my coming home at night, and unknown to me she had made definite plans to leave me when the children were older.

Along the way someone got me to go to a Sunday night fellowship group at the church. Brother, this was not for me. In no uncertain terms I told the folks they could have their little spiritual evening, and I would go my merry way.

But we remained friends with one of the couples in that group, and one night at dinner they started talking about all the wonderful things that were happening in it. I liked these people a lot, so I couldn't doubt the truth of what they were saying—regardless of how foreign it was to my own experience.

They invited us to the first meeting in a three-night series on "Faith at Work" being sponsored by our congregation. I fully expected the usual Bible-waving, tambourine-shaking, "you are damned" type of meeting which had always been so repulsive to me. But I went—skeptically, to be sure.

Much to my relief I discovered that the people who addressed us that evening were down to earth and ordinary. They told simply but with vigor how God had entered their lives. The first speaker was a colonel in the Air Force, and I was deeply impressed with his story.

Then a couple from our own church talked—one of the couples I had locked horns with a year before on the question of the fellowship meetings. What they said was surprising and impressive, and I kept thinking the girl was looking directly at me through the whole thing. (Later I found out she was trying to figure out what I was doing there at all.)

Slowly I became aware of an odd feeling—a series of mixed emotions which I cannot fully describe. There was sadness, joy, and some confusion. Suddenly I knew what I would say if I should be called on to address the group. The words were crystal clear in my mind: *God once again has His hand on my shoulder, only this time I know it.*

After the meeting was over I fled the room. I needed to get some air and collect myself. In the car my wife said, "What did you think of it?" It took me several minutes to answer. Finally I said, "You know, listening to these people made me feel like I've been riding on their coat-tails. Look at all the blessings I've had all my life, and never once have I thanked God for them."

My emotions were boiling and I couldn't say any more. This bothered me, too. Here I was, a grown man, working among men all the time, and what's more I'd knocked around the world and been through plenty—but I was thrown into a tailspin by a few people standing up and saying what Christ meant to them.

When I got to bed, it was as if every emotion had been drained out of me. I felt empty, hollow. I said, "Christ, take me."

No thunderbolts. No lightning. I fell asleep.

But the next morning I woke up to a different world. There was a peace of mind, a calmness, a confidence. I went to work walking on air. Every single thing that ordinarily bothered me I just took in stride. There were a couple of men that I'd decided only two days before should have "the book thrown" at them. Now I couldn't do it.

I called them to my office, sat them down. Instead of bawling them out with an endless string of profanity (and incidentally, my every sentence was punctuated with swear words up to that point), I told them quietly that I was a Christian, and wanted to run the place as a Christian. There were some pretty surprised reactions.

A few minutes later a man who had just returned to the post office after several weeks in the hospital got his work fouled up. Instead of exploding, I just went over and did the job, with him helping me. He said, "What's the matter with you? You're different."

This wasn't just a one-day thing. My whole attitude toward work and method of work changed. And I'm not afraid any more to speak of my relationship with God, even on the job.

My wife found a very happy change in me. Our home life changed overnight. Before, we never talked—now we talk endlessly, and God is in our conversations. Just the other night we had company, and the chance came to tell these folks, who are Catholics, "Every good thing that has happened in our lives lately has been the result of prayer."

The woman's face lighted up. "You don't know how happy it makes me to hear you say that," she said. "Sometimes I think people think we Catholics are crazy because we believe in answered prayer."

I just can't get over the dynamic quality of this Christian life I find myself praying all the time. And it's not me, for I never did these things before. It has to be the Holy Spirit working in me. He's made me able to go to people whose feelings I have hurt, and apologize to them.

For the first time in years I feel close to my three sisters. Just a few days after my rebirth I had an irresistible impulse to go to see one of my sisters, whom I'd neglected for a long time. I told her everything that had happened to me. Next day she called my wife and my other sisters and said in all her life she'd never felt so close to her brother. No need to emphasize what that meant to me.

These are the deep things that have turned my world upside-down. I find reality in prayer, enjoyment in the Bible. Now I find I can love people I didn't even like before. I go into my Sunday school classroom with new inspiration and vigor. No longer does the "big bear" rage home from the office every evening and make his family's life miserable. Yes, God has His hand on my shoulder once again, only this time I know it and this time I am going to hold it there. —*March, 1962*

Parts of Otto Schwarz's story were first narrated into a tape recorder under the probing questions of a colleague and myself one wintry day early in 1962. We were completely disarmed by Otto's sincerity and his obvious desire not to exaggerate or mislead, but to relate his experiences in the most accurate and constructive way possible. I met him a number of times afterward and that first impression never faded. He is the sort of guy for whom one should reserve terms like "salt of the earth." Whatever Otto is doing today, I am sure God's hand is still on his shoulder.

PART TWO
■

WHERE DO I GO FROM HERE?

The new road is unfamiliar and hazardous. For someone living the great adventure, pressures mount on all sides to retreat or to conform.

Here are men and women who have found the new road well worth traveling, in spite of inner doubts and outer pressures. Their experiences raise provocative questions regarding the life of a pioneer on "The Way"—questions which each of us must answer for himself. Come: let's explore together . . .

Chapter 12

■

HOME AT LAST

by Mary Fleuty
Housewife, Cooksville, Ontario

My world began to collapse around me. I thought nobody knew that I was drinking too much. But I knew, and I was weighed down with guilt.

Outwardly I put up a good front. I sent my children to Sunday school and church but I didn't go. My husband Byrnes and I would go to a party and drink moderately, but I could hardly wait to get home and get drunk. I had become an alcoholic and it almost cost me my home and family, and even my life.

Something inside kept saying, "Don't do this. It isn't right." I was having blackouts. I couldn't remember where I'd been, or what I'd done with the car. But I kept right on and hated myself for it.

Then people began to talk and Byrnes's business fell off. One of the children became seriously ill. I caught my own son looking at me with obvious hatred. I hoped and prayed that I would die.

How had I gotten this way? My father had tried so hard to raise me right. But Mother had died when I was five years old. Father was left with four children to raise. He was a wonderful man, a good Christian, and did the very best he could for us. But because he couldn't handle four little ones, he farmed us out to different homes, and as a result we were never very long in one place.

This went on for more than two years, until my father one day informed me that he was going to remarry. I was thrilled. It would be wonderful to have a mother again. All four of us children were tremendously excited about coming home.

I loved my stepmother. At first she did all the things I thought a mother should do. Where I had had hand-me-down clothes, she made me new ones. She made me feel wonderful. Then something else happened. She had children of her own. Naturally, time had to be spent on them, and again I felt rejected. I wasn't getting the things I'd been getting. I began to resent this new family and especially my stepmother. I rebelled at every turn. Feeling protective toward my brothers, I wasn't going to let them be set aside either.

Jealousy and hate grew in me and I vowed there would come a day when I would live my own life and nobody could tell me what to do. I lived for that moment, which came sooner than I expected.

At fifteen I quit school. I was sick and tired of doing dishes and cleaning house for a family of six and five hired men (my father had a cheese factory). I came home one day, threw my books on the table, and announced I was going to get a job. My father said it was up to me and didn't argue the point at all.

I left home and got a job. It was depression time and wages weren't very good during those years. Though I left home of my own free will, I did miss the things there, especially the fellowship of my brothers. However, I was determined to live my own life and not complain to anyone.

My father was a godly man. We had prayer in our home

every day. He took us to Sunday school regularly and to church. He saw that we had spiritual food, though he was too busy to spend time with us individually. One thing he insisted on was that no child of his would ever touch a drop of liquor or smoke a cigarette. This was really built into me.

And even though I was now out on my own, I vowed that I would never take a drop of liquor or smoke a cigarette as long as I lived and nobody who ever came in contact with me would do it either.

At seventeen I married Byrnes. He was older than I and seemed like a father to me. Byrnes was raised in a different kind of home from mine. As he grew up, his parents said, "If you want to take a drink, bring it into the house; don't go out behind the barn." So all his life he had drunk in moderation.

After our marriage I set to making Byrnes's life just as miserable as I'd made my stepmother's. I laid down the rules and said, "Don't you dare take a drink. Smoke your cigarette someplace else."

Two children came along and all through this time Brynes never took a drink to my knowledge. Then I had a very serious illness, was in the hospital for three months, and in bed at home for weeks after that. The doctor came in one day and said, "I really think you should have something to build you up. I would prescribe a glass of port before each meal and you know, it wouldn't hurt you to smoke a cigarette once in a while to help your nerves." Both of these things went against the grain, but I thought, *Well, if the doctor prescribes it, maybe I'd better.*

I'd been in bed quite a long time and was anxious to get up and so Byrnes very gladly got port and even bought me a pack of cigarettes. He poured my first glass. I tasted it and liked it. What had been the matter with me, yelling at him that he couldn't have a drink? I had another and soon I was telling

Byrnes it would be just fine if he went out and bought himself a case of beer.

Soon I was out of bed and not too long afterward we were invited to a party. I'd always reneged on these things before. I was "holier than thou" and thought others were no good. However, I went to the party and learned, as I went to others, that I could drink twice as much as anybody else. I liked this. The more I drank, the more I wanted. Every day I could think of a reason why we should have a party or go to one.

And so I started the long slide downward until my world collapsed, and I knew that I was a hopeless alcoholic.

But it didn't stop my drinking. Byrnes and I decided we would move. We chose the town of Cooksville, Ontario. We were going to sell the old business in Embro where we were and get out. People could just go on talking. We'd run our own lives.

We bought a house in Cooksville, but we couldn't sell the one in Embro. For two years the new house sat empty, with all the money we'd put into it completely wasted as the kids in town literally tore it apart. And still I went on drinking.

One night I went to a party with a strange feeling that something was going to happen. I couldn't seem to get into the swing of things. As I stood with a glass in my hand, a conviction came over me, *Put it down. You've had your last drink.* I tried to argue, but after this happened three times, I obeyed the impulse.

I couldn't explain it. God never entered my mind. I didn't say anything to anyone there, but when I got home, I told Byrnes what had happened and said, "I know I'm never going to take another drink." And from that day to this neither one of us has had a drink or even the desire for one.

I got up the next morning and vowed to get in touch with a minister. My pride was involved because, although I lived in a small village, I couldn't remember the minister's name. Through the telephone operator, I got hold of the Rev. Francis Yardley and asked him to come over. We talked, and he prayed with me. For six weeks I sat on his doorstep every single day. I never left his home without a prayer and in all that time he never once condemned me or gave advice. I saw in him and his family pure love in action.

During one of those visits, Frank felt that I was ready to commit my life to Christ. He prayed for me and I followed suit. When the prayer ended I felt cleansed and renewed inside. I was full of joy. Everything looked different—even my home.

I began to go to fellowship groups and get exposed to people who were filled with the love of God. Some of the first people I met were Canon Quintin Warner and Ralston Young. I was eager to get going. I remember saying to Ralston, "Gee, I've been a Christian for a month and a half and the Lord hasn't given me a thing to do." And he replied, "When you become usable, God will use you." It was then that I realized that I had to start in and learn how to live the Christian life. I began with my Bible, with all the books I could find, and with the "Twelve Steps of Alcoholics Anonymous."

We were still living in Embro. For a year and a half we had been partially packed and ready to move. I unpacked everything in the house and said, *Well, God, we'll stay here.* Within a week a buyer came and we sold the place and moved. It was miraculous the way it happened when I let go and let God take over. We didn't even advertise. Previously we'd advertised from Vancouver to Nova Scotia.

For seventeen years I'd "wandered in the desert" and hurt a lot of people. Restitution now became necessary, but it wasn't as hard as I thought it would be. I went to my stepmother and apologized and she lovingly accepted me. We had a wonderful friendship until she died eleven years later.

We had to rely entirely on God to get the house in Cooksville finished, even up to the painting. We'd run out of money. We went to see a friend who once had said he would help. He had been very ill in a hospital. When we asked about the paint, he said he could do nothing. After we'd been there awhile, we had a chance to witness and to win him for Christ. Suddenly he said he would not only get us the paint but put it on for us.

So our home got painted on the outside, and on the inside it became a haven for God's children. We've seen wonderful things happen. The doors are open twenty-four hours a day to anyone— those with broken homes and broken hearts, alcoholics and drug addicts. The one thing I asked was that God would give me love for these people, so that I could look beyond the sin and see the person as God sees him. It doesn't happen all the time. I get tired and irritable and suddenly I'm running the show again.

But then I remember a verse of Scripture God gave me years ago. I woke up three times in one night hearing these words, "Seek ye first the Kingdom of God and His righteousness and all these things shall be added unto you." I didn't even know it was from the Bible. But the very next night Byrnes and I went to church in Toronto and they were the first words to come from the minister's mouth.

Now when I recall Jesus' words, and let Him take charge, He does. And once again His love flows through me to the people He sends to share our home.   —*October, 1963*

Sometimes the things people don't say about themselves are as important as the things they do say. This is not necessarily lack of candor, but simply that we don't see ourselves as others see us. Mary Fleuty, for example, may not be aware that she has a warmth and delicacy, a spontaneous show of love and acceptance, which far transcends what she says about her spiritual journey. Long years before I met Byrnes and Mary, I knew of them through the printed word. When at last we were introduced, my first reaction was, "Of course . . . of course. It's all true!"

Chapter 13

∎

MY NAME IS PEACE

by Irene Munagian

Housewife, Chicago, Illinois

One beautiful autumn afternoon my husband and I were driving from Chicago to a weekend Christian "retreat." As we approached our destination, I reminded Nick that we should be ready to help out, since we were experienced at "this sort of thing." Perhaps we could share our Christian growth with the newcomers.

I reflected on how I had come to know Christ, first as Comforter, then as Guide, and finally as Saviour. He had begun to change my life, and I wanted to know Him better.

Arriving at the camp, we found that the planning team and early arrivals were meeting together. We hastened to join them, and soon it was time to go "around the circle," introducing ourselves and saying whatever was on our hearts and minds. I rather startled myself by saying I was concerned about my inability to witness to Christ in the spoken word.

The second surprise came that evening during our first "talk-it-over" session. I found myself sitting next to Rosalind Rinker, who headed one of the small groups. She began the introductions, and I asked to be last to speak, feeling no particular inspiration. By the time it got around to me I was bored at long-winded introductions, thinking, *I'm not going to get anything out of this.*

One man mentioned anger and resentment. This started a reaction in me, and though it was time to close the meeting, I
blurted out, "My heart is pounding now that it's my turn."

I spoke of the two parts of me at war with each other, and
how I had always hoped some day to live up to the meaning of
my name (*Irene* means *peace*). I told of the anger in me, and
the impatience that kept me from being what I wanted to be.
And I said that God helped me to overcome anger and impatience
so that I was not troubled by them as before, but that I still had
occasional bursts of temper that were upon me before I had a
chance to pray, and that I could in no way prevent them. I intended to stress that these outbursts were much reduced and
rarely occurred—that God had indeed helped me by taking away
the *feeling* of anger, not merely giving me control over it.

Two men volunteered suggestions, which surprised me even
more. One mentioned that God had enabled him to control his
own temper. Both felt the answer lay in prayer. I resented their
"interference," feeling that they had missed the whole point—
that I had *already* been cured, and that an occasional outburst
was not worth bothering about. I was perturbed that my testimony wasn't accepted at face value, and hastened to set it right,
not listening to any reply.

That night I slept poorly. Toward morning I awoke and pondered the day's events. I was sure God had a purpose in putting
my "testimony" of anger into unbidden words. I knew that the
group had not mistaken my need, though I admitted none. I was
afraid of what He was telling me. I fell asleep, and dreamed. In
my dream, I became angry at a child. Then I was alone, seething
with rage. I felt I was near to bursting.

Nothing seemed to happen the next day. The talk was dull, or
disconnected, or too "intellectual." I made no effort to understand or contribute. During the workshop period my husband
and I "played hooky," taking a walk and going for a drive.

On Sunday morning the Bible study in my group appeared to offer me nothing. I didn't suspect what the verses of John 15 would come to mean to me before the next two days were over.

The worship was about to begin when I suddenly became quiet inside. I yielded at last to the voice within, and the clamoring thoughts and feelings that pressed upon me were stilled. I said quietly, "Lord, if there is anything You can say to me today, with only this short time left, if there is yet something for me at this conference, let Thy will be done."

I had forgotten there was to be a healing ceremony with the laying-on of hands before the close of the worship service.

And then it was time. We were reminded that this was for complete healing—spiritual and emotional, as well as physical. Not knowing what part of me was hurt or sick, I was sure I needed help.

The healing service was completely new to me. We came in groups of four to a place in front of the congregation. I walked up to a chair and sat down, bowing my head, stilling my thoughts. When my turn came, four men laid their hands upon my head and shoulders. The young minister in charge held my head in his hands and prayed for me, and the prayers of the people present joined with his to invoke the power of the Holy Spirit.

His words startled me. I thought at first that he had me confused with someone else, and then I thought he must have his words mixed up, and then finally I accepted it—all in a matter of moments. For what he said shook me to the center of my being. He reached into the depths of my soul to speak of something that was troubling me unaware—the unlovingness of a member of my family. Then he prayed that I might be healed of "always having to be right." Finally, he prayed that I might be healed of the anger in me, and enabled to love.

Is it any wonder that I was shaken? The very expressions were mine, though I had neither thought nor spoken them. Yet I was able to accept this as something God wanted to reveal to me. I remained in a rather shaky condition throughout the healing service, the noon meal, and leave-takings, knowing that something tremendous had happened and was still happening.

On the long way home I told my husband what had happened, sorting out certain memories and habits of my life, and marveling at the new insights. Having accepted the *fact* of unlovingness and rejection, I began to see the *cause* of it, and some of the results as they appeared in my personality.

That night I lay awake. One part of me quaked; another part calmly thought, *I may have to go through a period of absolute breakdown in order to be healed completely.* But even if this happened, I knew God would see me through to the light on the other side.

I slept. During the night I awoke, feeling sick and apprehensive, but somehow God reassured me and I put myself in His hands. He seemed to lift me up and carry me, and I fell asleep once more, unafraid.

The following day was spent delving more deeply into myself— what made me the person I had become. I read the New Testament and devotional books I had brought home from the conference.

By the second day I had calmed down somewhat, and was then led to penetrate more deeply into the "why" of me. By evening it was clear that I must trust Jesus Christ alone to help. "He is the way," the books agreed. I believed this with all my heart, but still did not know how to go about giving myself to Him. I wanted to "get it over with," and know that His Spirit would flow unhindered through me as pictured so clearly in John 15. Silently I spoke the words of commitment, but even though I accepted it as done, I didn't know how much more remained for me to see.

By the third day I believed that God *had* healed the thing in me that prevented the love of His Son from taking control. I thought that I must *believe* I was healed before the results of healing would manifest themselves. Gradually the fruits would appear and I would find myself witnessing to the love of Christ, or so I told myself in my impatience.

And then I smugly began to think that perhaps I was already rid of the anger. After all, I hadn't felt angry for at least three days. Almost immediately, as though waiting for this moment, anger reared its ugly head and took over the reins once more. I was helpless and in tears at this demonstration of my weakness; even angry at my inability to do anything about the tide of resentment. I called upon God for help.

Though I still believed that He had rooted out the cause, I now feared that there was a further process of painful healing to go through. Already I realized that my life was based on being sufficient unto myself. Both my father and mother had taught me that I must learn to be dependent upon no one, but I was discovering the weakness of this foundation. Now I was forced to see how my every thought, my knowledge of right and wrong, my ideas of good and evil, were rooted in this false foundation, *and that they might all be wrong.*

This, then, was where the trouble lay. I must be willing to give up every bit of myself to Christ. None of my attitudes, beliefs, emotions, or ideals could remain. *All* must be turned over to Him. I knew this would leave me nothing of myself, and I rather liked some parts of me. But the Lord had made me see the likelihood of error, and I couldn't doubt what He had so clearly shown me. I was afraid to let everything go, but so desperate for help that I was finally impelled to break down and cry, "All right, then. Take me."

Immediately I saw myself handing over a limp, soiled, useless rag, saying, "That's me. I don't want me any more and I don't know why You do—but here I am." Suddenly I felt as though

I had stepped completely outside myself. It was like leaving a house that had grown cold and lonely. I was still frightened, afraid that I would have to wander alone through "waterless places" until Christ called me back to a house put in order for my return.

And then the miracle happened. How it happened I do not know, but somehow I had become a little child, untaught, unafraid. The woman I had been was gone, and I felt a pang of pity for her, thinking, *Poor soul.*

Jesus Christ was Lord and Master. He loved me, and had always loved me. He would teach me all I would need to know. His constant care would protect me from any danger I might face in the future. As a child must, I put my trust in Him alone. My old foundation of self-sufficiency had crumbled into dust. He was my new foundation, my rock.

After all the months since this took place I am still fully aware of what it means to be a "born-again" Christian. I know that Jesus Christ will never let me go. My name is Peace.

—April, 1961

Rarely does a manuscript excite me as much as did this one from Mrs. Nick Munagian. After reading it, I turned to a fellow staff member and said, "Here is a woman who, in the space of a few days, went through an experience comparable to five years of psychoanalysis—and without a doctor!" So startling was the change reported in the story that we waited many months before publishing it, to make sure that it was "real." It was indeed real, as present correspondence with Irene further testifies. She and her husband continue to take active spiritual leadership in their community.

Chapter 14
■

A KING-SIZE RESENTMENT
by Paul M. Offill, Jr.
Assistant to the Headmaster, Director of Development, Wooster
School, Danbury, Connecticut; formerly in business in Pittsburgh

As we drove downtown the other night, I found myself saying
to Bill, "I wish you could meet him. I think you'd like him after
you got to know each other." And then: "Listen to who's talking!
Imagine my saying that a couple of years ago."

Many months before this conversation I was talking to Bill
about the same man, the president of our small company, and
saying something like this: "My worst problem, Bill, is my job
and how to handle my boss. He's a tight-fisted, stubborn, self-
made man who can only see doing things *his* way. He makes
snap judgments about people and things and is usually wrong.
He antagonizes customers and prospects by his rough approach,
and frankly, I don't know how much longer I can take it."

Yes, I had a king-size resentment against this man. As director
of sales, I disagreed with him regularly on sales policies, especially
in the direction of the salesmen in the field who supposedly were
my responsibility. I was losing interest and incentive, and worse,
I was no longer loyal to the company.

Married for sixteen years, with three children, I had material
success, with flashes of deep love and happiness along the way,
but now I felt an undercurrent of uneasiness in many areas of

my life. I seemed to be losing my touch. It did not occur to me to ask for help.

Then a near tragedy involving long and horrible suffering to someone very close to me, a sledge-hammer blow that stopped me in my tracks, forced me for the first time to look deep inside myself. I found a vacuum there instead of faith in God. But the night of the accident, a night of soul-searching and crying for help, marked the end of the old existence and the beginning of a new, wonderful, sometimes hard and painful life.

All through those agonizing first nights and days after the accident, I stood on the sidelines and watched someone I loved fight the battle for survival with the sure faith that God was beside her. This obvious faith shocked me into a growing awareness of God's love for me. I was also mightily impressed by the power of the prayer which poured into that little hospital from Pittsburgh friends and prayer groups.

Only a few weeks later I started on the search for greater faith, first making prayer a regular part of my life. I found fellowship and real concern in the church that I joined. As a member of a neighborhood prayer group I gained spiritual strength. Marriage took on new meaning with a close understanding never experienced before, and in our struggle to develop family devotions each of us has become conscious and aware of Christ in our home. We have made many new friends and are finding that the sharing of the Spirit is one of the richest and most rewarding experiences of our lives.

It wasn't long after I started on this search when I knew I had to face up to the job situation—the problem which was still a corrosive factor in my life. First came prayer that I might better understand and experience Christian love toward the man I worked for. I began to suppress the constant irritation caused by his reactions to my suggestions and by the operation of the Pittsburgh office.

Then the boss came to Pittsburgh, and I was with him night and day for a week. I made it a point to avoid the controversial subjects which usually ended in argument. For the first time we talked about our families: I learned that his daughter was a muscular dystrophy patient and heard about his sons and his hopes for them. In this revealing week, it began to dawn on me that perhaps we could find a basis for friendship.

Much later, while our relationship was being improved, and, incidentally, our business in the Pittsburgh office, too, a serious problem came up regarding major salary raises for our salesmen. Unless these raises came through there was danger that our sales organization would fall apart. Six months before, I would have handled this with an abrupt request for immediate action. If my recommendations had been overruled, I would have bitterly suggested to the men that they resign and find work elsewhere.

Fortunately, the boss was scheduled to come to Pittsburgh again, and I was able to postpone a decision until I could have a personal session with him on this very real business crisis. When the opportunity came, I made certain that we would have two hours for uninterrupted discussion in his hotel room. Then instead of making my usual antagonistic approach I spent the first hour telling him about the Pittsburgh Experiment and one particular men's prayer group which was familiar with my job situation and which had prayed about this present conference and the right solution to our problems. I told him that I myself had prayed that the right decision would be reached.

In turn he now surprised me by saying that he, too, had prayed that a way would be found for closer cooperation between us, and after another hour's analysis a satisfactory solution was reached. It was further agreed that we would have quarterly conferences in the future to talk out business conditions and problems. Today we both pray in preparation for these meetings, and knowing this fortifies my confidence.

The search for faith is still going on, but I now have a beginner's vision of what life can be like with God at my side. With God now in the work situation, furthermore, I find it easier to focus on other areas. I realize increasingly how much I need Him in every aspect of my life.   —*March, 1957*

Paul Offill is a breezy Episcopalian who combines a great zest for life with a great love of God. His business acumen and expertise have opened many doors, and have helped him to fulfill a spiritual ministry in Pittsburgh and elsewhere for a good many years. My first editorial contact with Paul came through his account of a life-sharing adventure he and his wife Elinor and several laymen from Washington had in a Baptist church in Kansas. The pastor of that church was Roger Fredrikson, and the lay witness and small groups experiment conducted that weekend has borne rich fruit in Roger's present pastorate in Sioux Falls, South Dakota. The ramifications of the story are too complex to go into here, but they give hints of authentic church renewal through the interaction in depth of committed laymen and pastors. Paul Offill is a pioneer in such renewal.

Chapter 15

∎

THE KEY

by Robert Walker
Editor, "Christian Life"

It was the summer before my senior year as a journalism major at Northwestern University, and I'd had a wonderful time relaxing, playing, and studying at a little cabin on the shore of Lake Superior.

But now it was September, and one by one all my neighboring campers had packed up and treked home. I had eagerly gone through all the philosophy books I'd brought along—required reading for the college year ahead—and now, with no one around to swim or fish with, I was at loose ends.

Well there *was* that Bible I had brought along (somewhere I had heard that anyone wishing to become a successful writer should know the English Bible), and so, reluctantly, I picked it up and started to read.

It didn't make sense, even when I tried to place it in the context of my upbringing in a Methodist home and church. As always, even the familiar Bible passages seemed to have nothing to do with my life, with the "real" world. My father, for example, was a man of sterling moral character, but never expressed his convictions to me, and his business life seemed completely divorced from his churchgoing, or "spiritual" life. Plainly, I was in a muddle.

It wasn't the first time I'd been in a muddle. When I left home for secondary school in Massachusetts, I left behind whatever restraints my home environment had provided. My principal occupations were football, wrestling, and track. Along with the stiff academic requirements of the school, this kept me fully occupied. Daily required chapel services found my body in the pew and my mind elsewhere!

During this time my father sold his business and moved to Chicago as a consulting engineer, and so when the time came for college I entered the University of Illinois. Here the new vistas of fraternity life and the anticipation of athletic achievement overwhelmed me.

Then came the rude awakening. First I discovered that I was simply not good enough to play varsity football. Then I began to suspect that life involved more than sheer physical and mental activity, and there seemed to be a restless spirit within me. The more I thought about this need for "spiritual fulfillment," the more I realized that in my present orbit I neither had it nor the possibility of finding it.

Bewildered, I talked with various professors, but most of them sloughed off my questions. The head of the philosophy department, however, was willing to spend time with me, and for hours we discussed the subject of peace of mind and heart. He admitted he did not have it, but he also admitted the possibility of finding it in some types of religious experience.

By the middle of my sophomore year it was clear that I had to leave the University of Illinois. I didn't know just why, but realized I was looking for something and not finding it.

The next two years can be described as a flight from reality. The small school to which I transferred was religion-centered, and clearly presented the answer I needed, but I was not ready for it. I did satisfy my desire to play football, but I was still "struggling in the wilderness."

Then I finally singled out journalism as the area in which I wanted to major, and transferred again, this time to Northwestern University. And that is how I happened to be sitting by the shore of Lake Superior that summer, trying to improve my knowledge of English and to get some sort of background understanding of the Bible.

As I sat turning the pages, it occurred to me that by reading aloud I might improve my diction. Propped against a big fir tree, I would read aloud for hours at a time, both from the Old and New Testaments.

The next thought that came was that since I was spending so much time with the Bible I should be trying to see what message it contained which seemed so significant to so many people. I was missing it completely, but I couldn't see any harm in keeping an open mind, and so in my heart I said, "God, if you are the Lord and this is your Word, I am willing to be shown."

I don't know at what point I actually began to pray in this fashion, but I am sure that as soon as I opened my mind to the Word of God, the Holy Spirit began to speak to me. I remember clearly one day writing to a friend, and mentioning the fact that I was reading the Bible. At that moment a tremendous desire came over me to share with this friend some of the thoughts that had been coming to me as I read. But I was unable to communicate to him what I had experienced.

As I think back now I do not believe there was any specific moment when I became aware that a change had taken place in me. I don't remember just when I thought I had become a Christian. But when I packed up to go back to school, about the middle of September, I knew that I was a different chap than I had been scarcely two weeks before.

When I got back to the campus, I went to see the dean of the Journalism School. "I think I had better drop out," I said.

"Why?" he asked in surprise.

"This summer I read the Bible. I don't know exactly what happened, but I think I'm what they call 'converted,' " I replied. "I suppose I ought to become a preacher, and that means entering seminary."

We discussed the matter fully, and in the end the dean persuaded me to stay on for the last year and graduate from Journalism School. "We need men with strong convictions in our field, too, you know," he said. "If you still want to go into the ministry later, I'm sure that will be possible."

From that point on the Lord has led me in a most faithful manner. I have made many mistakes, but I have never failed to find that the Word of God has been the key to successful Christian living. Not only that, but it is the key to enabling the Holy Spirit to demonstrate through us to others the power of the new life in Christ.   —*September, 1960*

At first it seemed presumptuous to ask a busy editor like Bob Walker to write his story for a "rival" magazine, but he didn't see it that way. Somehow he found the time to do it, and his account of an idealistic but ambitious young man coming to terms with God and life through reading the Bible made a valuable contribution to "the magazine of Christian experience." It illustrates graphically the simple power of the Word of God to affect profoundly an agile but open mind. Warm ties of friendship between Bob Walker and his "Christian Life" organization and the FAITH AT WORK staff continue to this day.

Chapter 16

■

FOUR THINGS FOR SURE

by Anne Standish

I am a widow. It has taken me two years to say it out loud, but I am. Occasionally I even qualify as a merry one. I am not old, I am not ugly—and I may well have thirty good years ahead of me.

I think it would be very comfortable to slip out of the business world where I earn my living, to say "yes" to a man of my kind who wanted to carry me home to mother his children or mind his manor. Remarriage was something my husband and I agreed on as a wise move for either of us, should death us part. But statistics imply that it is not a very likely possibility, so it is reasonable to consider my major problems and their solution.

There are four thing I know for sure about widowhood. First, *I have a greater need than ever before to be reassured that I am a child of God,* capable of receiving real power from His Spirit for all of the new requirements. Second, *I still have a deep need to share with another human being* in an honest intimate fellowship—to know, and to be known as I am. Third, *I must have genuine purpose for my new life,* day by day, and on through the years. And fourth, *I have a need for masculine presence.* All of the tender toughness that surrounded me for years is suddenly cut off, leaving a great void.

I will never forget the strange, comforting presence of Christ during the moments and days immediately following my husband's death—as I drove through the streets, walked about the house, lay in my bed at night, talked with my friends. This comfort was and is so deep and reassuring that it is often misread by onlookers. Some sadly shake their heads and lament, "She couldn't really have loved him."

I remember trying to explain the wondrous love of God to a Christian friend who insisted she didn't have the kind of faith that could see her through her husband's death. I tried to use the analogy of a river bottom as the course of life; and the water flowing over the deeps as well as the shallows as the constant love of God.

We have little idea of the depths of His love, until we hit an unforeseen drop in the course of life. Then all of a sudden we realize He hasn't just spread a thin layer of love over the top of life, leaving the deep holes empty and dry. When life is gouged by deep loss, let me assure you from my own experience that He is just as faithful as His promises. His care and love have flooded into my "drop-offs," often even before I knew they existed. It has also been good for me to see others know these same certainties, for I have watched God do for them in their sorrow the same things He did for me.

As I think over the time since the very first morning I sat beside my beloved, and knew with a calm dread clarity that he was no longer there, a second need looms large. I need someone human with whom I can intimately share. I recall receiving two color pictures in the mail, on the very day of the funeral. They had been taken of the two of us on our last holiday together. I wanted to show them to him, but I realized with a sinking sensation that it was impossible. Since then others have shared this same feeling with me.

A dear friend attended a dinner and heard the toastmaster tell several stories that her husband would have enjoyed. How wonderful it used to be to go home and curl up beside him and retell such funny stories. But he was no longer there. And the reality of his death stung throughout every fiber of her consciousness.

Another friend, ten days after her husband's death, was seized with an illogical fear that she was losing her eyesight. It paralyzed her relationship to God, and the world closed in on her as a dark tunnel. When we had time together, we put our arms around each other and cried, and in the quiet privacy that followed, she poured out her heart, and was able to see her fear for what is was—only a shape without substance. This kind of fear is common to those of us who have been deeply bereaved. We need someone to hold us quietly and closely as we pour out the worries that so easily clog our pipeline of freedom to God and to our associates.

What a gracious gift prayer becomes as a perceptive friend offers not only a shoulder and an ear, but a praying heart. To talk to the Father with someone who cares enough to look at me as a person, with both empty places and full ones, is a glory that passes all others. Not stiff, wordy petitions, but spontaneous snatches of genuine three-way conversation, sometimes even without words. I remember the first time someone really prayed *with me* rather than *for me*. My heart was so melted with deep appreciation that I wept, for what deeper gift can one share with a friend than the gracious presence of God Himself?

The third need requires a great deal of time and patient watching. I need to know what purpose there is in my continuing to live. I had been a helpmate, a responder, a follower. Suddenly I was pushed into an entirely new role. I had to lead, to initiate, to set the pace. But the deadly thought nagged: "I don't know who I am. I don't know what I can do. I was born to be a wife, a helpmate. Now what is my role?"

Often the mocking answer echoes hollowly through the day:

"You are nothing now. There's no longer any reason for you to try. You don't want to get hurt again, anyway. Pull out. Withdraw. Lie low." This is what happens when I lose sight of my uniqueness in the mind of the Maker.

Sometimes at this point I come back to the Psalms and realize that people felt this way centuries ago; or I may open the Gospels and marvel at Christ's concern for individual persons. Perhaps I will need to pour out my grief all over again to some friend who cares enough to bring human warmth to melt and release the hidden spring.

Whatever I do, I must always come back to the point where I face the fact that I am *me*—unique, uncopied, custom-designed. And my purpose did not end when my husband's life did. I used to think people would eventually just drop me, because all of the wit and intelligence and know-how belonged to my beloved, not to me.

Now I know that my married period molded, sanded, and shaped me into the woman I now am. My new purposes will build out from the person that my husband helped to create. But he has been promoted, and I have walked into a new chapter without him. I am no longer married. (This is one of the hardest things to say, but must eventually be said by all of us.) My book is not finished; I am still the leading lady and I cannot walk out.

Sometimes I feel a great restless burden of unleashed love. Sometimes I weep, for there seems to be no place to spend it anymore. But I have learned to hand it to God, and then to open my eyes to see whom He will bring to me.

Everywhere I look I see pinched, crumpled-down, pushed-aside, locked-away people. Some of them will be specially marked for me. I pray that God will create in my home a warm climate of love and acceptance that will draw new friends and old into my own experience of His merciful kindness. This is not a simple life, but it is one jammed with real purpose, a sense of destiny, and an exciting expectation of guidance for every day.

The fourth lack brought on by widowhood—the need for masculine presence—is the trickiest to accept, for society has built stern, unbending walls, and only a few know how to love wisely or well enough to defy the old fable that widows are out to get somebody else's man. Twentieth-century society comprehends very little of what it means to give real love and tenderness to a person of the opposite sex without reading into the gesture an illicit quality.

Those of us who have had the bonds of marriage broken by death have a far greater need for companionship, conversation, and sincere compliment, than we do for sex *per se*. What kind of love is it that accepts a married couple in the deepest sense of friendship, but turns its back when death leaves the woman alone, making her feel as though she were worth nothing by herself?

It is almost silly how much of a lift one of my husband's friends can give me with a small compliment! "You know, the grayer you get, the prettier you are!" Or, "I've been admiring that hat in front of me all morning; if I'd stopped to think I'd have known it could only be you underneath it!" Such a comment brings fresh sparkle, and may lift a whole day; yet it doesn't cost the giver one cent.

God never did ordain that woman live only with woman. When Adam was lonely, God made for him Eve, not another Adam. Why then is it not normal for a bereaved woman to profit by the gentle teasing and toughness of the few men who dare to follow Christ's great commandment, and thus concern themselves with their good friend's widow?

Some women are hurt deeply by old friends who are too insecure to know what to say or how to act. We adjust in various ways. One of my friends solved the problem by taking a course in practical nursing after her husband died, then finding a job in the men's ward at the local hospital. Others are deeply appreciative of an occasional phone call, a significant question, an invitation to join the old group as an individual in her own right.

There is a great void in the sensible consideration of this problem that exists among the growing number of women who have lost their husbands. Women are allowed to help us in so many ways, and we are grateful. Men, who often are very perceptive of loneliness, usually have no idea how they should help. Some see the problem as a deadly danger, therefore flee from it, scared to death; others view it as an opportunity, and exploit it; a few recognize it as one need in a whole spectrum of human needs, and act to meet it through the law of Christian love. The latter need not only the Holy Spirit, but the generous, loving cooperation of their unjealous wives.

As for me, I am grateful for the obvious and continuing stream of God's messengers in my life. "My God shall supply *all* your needs, according to His riches" includes provision of all needs—the temporal ones we haven't even mentioned here, as well as the complex intangible ones that make the difference between just existing and living abundantly.

I cannot feel that widowhood was intended to bind us to unbroken bleakness of suffering and grief. We need to open our windows to Heaven to discern God's fresh new pattern for our lives. "It is to freedom we have been called . . . plant your feet firmly then," says Paul, "within the freedom that Christ has won for us . . . you should be free to serve each other in love."

—*October, 1964*

Once in a blue moon someone comes along who is able to express quite dispassionately but with great perception what it means to have the bottom drop out of life through the loss of a loved one. Anne Standish (a pseudonym) is such a person. Her story about adjusting to a life of widowhood is an example of clear-eyed faith at its best, and speaks to the condition of widows and widowers of all ages. Incidentally, in the years since this article was written, "Anne Standish" has carved out a new career. Though still quite young, she has not remarried.

Chapter 17

■

THIS IS MY LINE

by Adolf Unger
Presbyterian Minister, Rockford, Illinois

I found my line—my life's work—in a soup-line.

Not all at once, of course. But something I heard from the fellow next to me led me, step by step, to the work I want to do for the rest of my life.

We were inching along, scores of us, toward the tables where we would receive a paltry amount of food, in one of the concentration camps in Java where I spent most of World War II.

"Not such a bad deal; is it?" said this character, a little hesitantly, but evidently wanting to make friends. I was shocked. Was he kidding?

What's good about it? I almost said, but checked myself, taking a long look at him. His eyes were twinkling, but I could see he was serious. "How do you mean, not so bad?"

"Well, for one thing, look at all the time we have."

Time! That was just the trouble. Some day, I supposed, the war would end, but how many months or years of meaningless waiting and suffering lay ahead? I had never thought of it as anything but a waste.

"Maybe some of the guys will make discoveries they never expected," he went on. "Maybe these will be the best years of our lives."

We got our soup and became separated in the mob, but I remembered him and watched to see how he spent this *time* he seemed to value so highly.

The only thing I noticed was that he apparently knew everybody and was *persona grata* with all the various groups in the camp. Short of stature, quick-witted, he was interested in people, adept at striking up friendly conversations. He had been a lawyer in civilian life, I learned. His name was Pieter Volten.

I really could use some of the time at my disposal; to think, to sort out the contradictions and confusions and problems that had come rushing into my life with the war, and see if I could make sense of them. That synthesis—that integration, whatever it was—would not come in a day, I knew, if it came at all. Maybe Pieter Volten knew what he was talking about.

Not that my upbringing had not been sound and satisfying. We had been a happy family, back home in Holland. Good schooling, plenty of outdoor life, companionship, comfortable circumstances. My parents went to no small pains to give their children a firm religious foundation. Had I been asked, even now after two years of war and seven years of church membership, whether I was a Christian, I probably would have answered "yes" without much hesitation.

Thinking it over during the long days and nights, I came to realize that my religion had never gone beyond an outward conformity, a respect for my parents and their beliefs—but I had no deep abiding conviction or faith which could set me free in spirit even though imprisoned in body.

Was that what Pieter Volten had? I wanted to find out, but first I would do more thinking and reading on my own. So, armed with a modern translation of the Dutch New Testament, and, providentially as I now see it, two copies of a Christian magazine which had found their way into the camp in the knapsack of a fellow-prisoner, I read and studied—prayed some, too. To my surprise and pleasure I discovered almost by accident that I was not alone in my pursuits. Shyly, we like-minded fellows came together in small groups and talked about God and prayer and a new world touched with the spirit of Christ. Without benefit of clergy or any other expert guidance, we nevertheless did learn from each other in those sessions. At least they gave me the impetus to keep up the search.

Soon I sought out Pieter again. I had decided he was a practicing Christian, and he would be sympathetic with my gropings. I told him as best I knew how what my friends and I were doing.

When I had finished, he seemed enthusiastic. "Good! Great!" he said. "But have you told this to the fellows who aren't interested?"

I was startled; I had had to overcome much diffidence in telling him, whom I expected to be interested; how could I go to the indifferent or antagonistic? It seemed to me an unnecessary invasion of my privacy.

Yet, looking at him, I could see a gentleness in him; he was not accusing me so much as inviting me. It was as if he hoped I would join him in some adventure in which he wanted companionship.

I mumbled something about not having time, and about not meeting the right kind of fellow.

"Did you have to wait in line today?" asked Pieter innocently.

Foolish question! That's about all we did in that cursed place—wait in line. But then again, not so foolish. He was getting at something.

I wished I had not opened this conversation; I tried to keep my face composed, lest it betray my feelings. But Pieter only added, "In each line there are always two men waiting to meet Christ—the one standing before you and the other behind you."

This was characteristic. Wherever Pieter stood, sat, or lay, he talked with men. I had thought the subject matter was just the usual topics of the day: the hunger, the rumors, the beatings, the deaths. And often that was so. But now I realized that it was not merely small talk, with Pieter. For he had found a way not only of bearing but almost *welcoming* the experiences; all this somehow did not crush him, as it did so many; it strangely enriched him. He had a certain quality of life as he moved about camp that intrigued people. When a man asked about it, Pieter would tell him simply the secret: rebirth through Christ. And he would go with him through the steps: taking stock of his life, giving it to God in repentance and faith, accepting forgiveness, and caring that others find the same experience.

He considered each man an individual in need of a special kind of friendship and help, all according to the other's personality, and the guidance of the Holy Spirit. When, later, I also began to try to help people, I wanted to move faster than this. "Dolf," said Pieter patiently, "Don't try so hard to convert——. It's God's work *through* you. When you do it that way, you will also avoid a second mistake: you will not any more talk beyond the experience of the other man, because God alone knows how much he can digest." Nevertheless, I noticed, sooner or later, Pieter himself managed to lead the talks to a verdict, where the other person had to make a choice. But he never separated Christ from ordinary life, knowing Him to be the only answer in life.

We were to be moved to Japan, and the evening before the move, we had a short meeting, sitting on discarded school benches. There were silent prayers, and we listened in our quiet period to the mysterious sounds of the tropical evening. Suddenly Pieter stood up and said: "The best years of our lives! All we have to do is to surrender ourselves to God each day, listen to Him each day, and care each day for one another."

It was that evening for the first time in my life I felt the clear touch of God. Someone seemed to say in my heart, "I need your witness, too, and your care for others. And I need them from now on." I think this happened then because I had never before ventured beyond a kind of embryonic surrender. Walking back to the barracks, I told Pieter what had just gone through my heart.

Two days later, we were on a Japanese ship bound for Japan. On arrival there, we were separated and, at the last moment, Pieter said, "The only further thing that can happen to us is that God may take us away for higher service—and then the communion with Him is completed." As he marched out with the men from his transport, he passed me and I heard him repeat: "Surrender—listen—care."

After we were liberated, a mutual friend told me Pieter had died, along with many others, of double pneumonia in that terrifyingly cold winter in Japan.

At the time, a few hungry and cold men in the Osaka camp prayed and thanked God for Pieter and the others then separated from us. Thus began a camp church, and for the first time I was actually sharing my faith publicly. It was far from perfect; there were mistakes each day, many things done in my own strength. But his last words to me, "Surrender—listen—care," have stayed with me.

So I found my line. It is my job for life, this ministry which began with Pieter and has now carried me through ordination here in America. Each day I try to begin that way, knowing there is no other beginning but surrendering to God, listening to God and the man He sends across my path this day, and caring deeply for the other, be that one my wife, my child, my friend, or a person unknown to me until that day. Dietrich Bonhoeffer says in *Life Together,* "I must meet [the other] as the person that he already is in Christ's eyes."

That was Pieter Volten's secret. Thank God he did not keep it to himself.   —*September, 1956*

Dolf Unger's story is one of many to come out of the misery of concentration-camp life in World War II. It recalls in a less tragic way the discoveries outlined by Ernest Gordon in Through the Valley of the Kwai. *Such tales portray vividly the Christian conviction that good can emerge from the ghastliest circumstances. At any rate, Dolf's heartfelt ministry is an example of "life out of death." He and his wife Berta are long-time participants in the fellowship of FAITH AT WORK; in fact, at one time Dolf was a member of the staff. He has recently carried on an effective parish ministry in Illinois, and as this is written he is preparing to take up new duties as a teacher and counselor in a New England school.*

Chapter 18

ROOM TO GROW

by Nancy Thompson
Housewife, Lake Zurich, Illinois

A house in the country was what we always wanted. Lee and I had grown up in the city where apartments were so close you could look right into your neighbor's windows. So when we heard about the little house in Lake Zurich with a price tag we could afford, we couldn't pass it up.

Here our children would have plenty of room to grow. Here they would be away from the dangers of the city. Little did we realize that there is danger everywhere—of one kind or another.

Tom was three, and baby Steve one week old, when we moved into our dream house. And for the next year or so, everything was fine. But babies grow into busy toddlers and toddlers into inquisitive little children who really keep you running. So after three years in the country with two active youngsters and no car to enable me to get away once in a while, I began to feel sorry for myself.

Lee and I had little time for each other as he always was working: improving the house, working overtime at his trade, doing odd jobs for neighbors to earn extra money. I appreciated having a responsible husband. But I wanted to have my cake and eat it too. I missed the companionship we had shared before.

Of course there was happiness, too. Tom and Steve were

123

healthy, affectionate boys—Tom as happy as could be with so many friends to play with on our street, and Steve content to follow him about adoringly. Everything was an adventure for Steve. The simple task of opening a stick of chewing gum would bring a light of anticipation to his smiling eyes as he would slowly, carefully peel off the paper.

Steve would wander confidently up and down our suburban street, walking or riding his beloved bike. I thought it was cute when, one day, he parked right in the middle of the road and the school bus had to stop so someone could get out and move him. I said to myself, *Now, there's a lad with self-confidence. He keeps the bus waiting until he's ready to move.*

People warned me about Steve's disregard for the right of way of the neighbors' cars on our road. *They will watch for him,* I thought, and naturally, they did.

It never entered my mind that everyone wouldn't be that careful, so Steve grew up thinking the world was just a big, bright, wonderful place to explore, where people interrupted their work and talked to you, where everyone was your friend, and where cars stopped and waited while you crossed the street.

The summer Steve was three and a half, Lee and I decided we would finally be able to manage a vacation by ourselves. We planned to spend the first week with the children, doing things together—picnics, the amusement park, the zoo. The second week would be just for the two of us. And that really appealed to me with my "poor me" attitude.

The first week went well. At the zoo the children were enchanted with the animals. I remember Steve swaggering up to the huge elephant as if he, Steve, were going to overwhelm him with his great size. At the amusement park, the last day of the "children's vacation," he strutted around proudly, as if to say, "Look out, World, here I come!" He did it innocently, without vanity. He felt secure in his little realm, and showed it.

That evening we stopped at my mother's house to say goodbye before we left on our long-awaited second honeymoon. The children begged to play outdoors. It was hot and we were all tired, so I agreed. I cautioned them to stay in front of the house until we could take them to the neighborhood park.

Ten minutes later Steve came in again to ask, "Are you going to take me to the park now?" I lit a cigarette and told him impatiently, "We'll be right there; now stay in front of the house and wait. Don't go into the street!"

"I won't, Mommy," he promised.

It seemed only an instant until I heard the screech of brakes. Lee dashed out the door. I followed, interested, wondering what could have happened. Then I saw Tom running toward me, crying. "My brother," he sobbed.

I ran to the crowd, pushed people aside, and saw Steve lying under the wheels of a big car. It seemed then as if I went on "automatic pilot," calmly directing the men to move the car back off him, asking someone for a blanket, asking if anyone had called the police and an ambulance.

Then I felt for his pulse, and dread slowly entered my heart. I couldn't find any pulse! He gasped. Blood started to flow from his mouth and nose, and he breathed—slightly. But he did breathe!

"Oh, thank God," I prayed, "let him live, please."

At the hospital we waited forty-five agonizing minutes for the verdict, knowing in our hearts what would happen, but clinging to hope and believing in miracles. When I saw the doctor's face, I knew what he was going to tell me. He said, simply, "He didn't make it."

Our smiling, singing, happy, and confident little boy was gone. Just that quickly.

The pain was indescribable—too painful to dwell on.

The questions kept hammering at us. Why? Why did we allow

him outside on a city street? Why didn't we train him that cars were dangerous? Why did he have to die? Why did God do this?

This was when we learned what it means to have friends. They took over completely—attended to funeral arrangements, cooked, cleaned, loved, and cared for us in a thousand different ways. And it didn't stop in a week or so. Someone would pop in at any hour "just to say hello" and look carefully at us to see that we were all right.

At such a time of bereavement, one may not seem to be listening, consciously, to what people are saying or know what they are doing. But words of sympathy and acts of love from the heart get filed away in your memory to be brought out and thought about in the lonely moments of retrospect.

I remember everything that was said to me. And I shall never again be embarrassed or afraid to say or express in some way my true feelings for a person.

But there was something I had to work out alone, or face a lifetime of self-pity and misery. Looking back over my life, I realized my relationship to God had been a surface thing. We would go to church once in a while; would drop the children off at Sunday school; I would pray when I thought of it. But the deep, close relationship wasn't there. I knew that it called for constant nourishment, study and effort, and I never really wanted that much to be a Christian.

And now this shattering, tearing experience found me with no preparation, nothing solidly built. My faith was like the house of straw the little pig confidently built. It blew apart at the first huff and puff. It was time to take a good look at myself and do some meditating.

I remember my mother-in-law's challenge to me when I screamed at her in my agony, "How can I stand it?" She answered, great tears streaming from her eyes, "You say you're a Christian; now prove it!"

I recall the quiet strength of our minister and the confidence with which he answered our searching questions. How I envied his faith!

I remember, too, the sermon we heard at a friend's church: "A mother and father stand at the casket of their young son. 'Why?' they ask. One of the reasons *might* be to bring them to God.

"For example," he continued, "the shepherd is trying to get his sheep over the other side of the field. He knows it is better for them there. He tries everything; coaxes, calls, but nothing will entice them. Then he picks up a little lamb and walks away. The mother follows, and soon the whole flock."

I thought, *God must really want us if He took such drastic measures to bring us to Him.* And so we turned to Him. We began to put our troubles on Him. We began to read our Bible. We started really to listen to the sermons at church.

I don't know when the idea hit me that if we allowed nothing but good to come of it, Steve's death would not be a waste. Through him, our life could have meaning and purpose.

So this is how we're trying to live. Our new baby is one example. Before Steve's death, another baby would have been just one more demand on me. Now I realize that's what I'm here for. This is the reason God created me.

We live anew in our children. Everything we do for them and teach them will be remembered and will reflect for generations to come in their children and grandchildren. We can determine the direction our society will take. It is solemn responsibility and a very important full-time job.

I thank God for my baby girl, for my son Tom who feels so protective toward her, for my husband who shared everything so completely. I am sure I could not have found this peace without him. I am thankful for the new look at life I have been given and, most of all, for Steve, whose death opened our eyes. I don't feel I have miraculously found all the answers to life or happiness. But I do feel confident that I am on the right path.

I will always remember what Steve proudly announced one day when he returned from Sunday school. There was firm conviction and a bit of wonder in his voice when he said, "God loves *me*." I know now that He loves me, too.   —*October, 1964*

The rain falls on the just and the unjust, and sooner or later in his lifetime everyone faces tragedy. How we react to disaster is one measure of the reality of our spiritual experience. Do we fall apart? Do we stoically grit our teeth? Do we see trouble as a judgment or punishment? Or, in times of stress, do we see the circumstances as something that gives us "room to grow"? Nancy Thompson's deeply moving story provides food for thought.

Chapter 19

∎

THIS BUSINESS OF FAITH

by Francis Patton
Lawyer, Former F.B.I. Agent, Businessman
Leesburg, Virginia

Some years ago I had an employee running a milk route, making deliveries from store to store, who was a nice young boy and whom I liked very much. One day one of his customers called and asked me to come out to her store. When I got there she told me that this young man had been "jacking tickets." In other words, when he sold five dollars worth of milk, he charged her five-fifty, and so on. She showed me a sheaf of tickets on which he had overcharged her.

I called the boy in and, in my best FBI training procedure, obtained from him a written confession. Because I really liked him, and also because he was a good salesman and we were short-handed, I said, "If you will go back to your customers and tell them what you have done, now that you have confessed to me, and say you are sorry and will not do it again, and will pay back what you have stolen from them—and if they are willing to have you as their route salesman, then I'm perfectly willing to have you remain on the job."

He did all these things and I stood behind him, confident that he would be a good salesman from that day on.

About two weeks later another customer in another part of his route called to tell me he had started cheating again. And we fired the boy.

Approximately a year after that I came into a tremendous religious experience. I came to know Jesus Christ, and turned my life over to Him with words like these: "Lord, You take my life and from this day on You run it." Frankly, I didn't know what it meant. I didn't have the slightest idea what I was doing, but I have been finding out.

The following August I ran into trouble with another route salesman, the best one we had. He was making about a hundred and fifty dollars a week—very good for selling milk from store to store. To my surprise and disappointment I discovered he had "jacked tickets" to the tune of about twenty dollars over a period of three months.

I called the young man in and said, "My boy, here are twenty tickets that you have jacked a dollar each. Now I want to know how many more there are." There were quite a number more.

Then I went on, "Now, you can tell me you're sorry and won't do it again, but that won't mean too much to me. If you ever want to get anywhere, on this job or any other, you're going to have to make peace not with Frank Patton, but with God."

We had quite a session together, and at the end of it the boy actually turned to the Lord Jesus in prayer, and asked forgiveness for the sin that had come in and was dominating his life. Then he went back to every customer and told what he had done, and set things right. He is still with us, and one of our best salesmen.

I am trying to point out how being a Christian has made me act differently in my business, and how situations can be resolved in a better way than I used to know.

But, you may say, this is an employer-employee relationship. What happens when it gets into another area—when my own pocketbook is threatened? I think that the minute we turn our lives over to Christ the devil gets busy and starts to figure out ways to show us what asses we are making of ourselves, and how nothing we do makes sense.

Here is an illustration. The milk business where I operate is highly competitive. We have a policy of not giving discounts to our customers. Finally the time came when we were faced with having to give a discount to the biggest chain of stores in the area—a chain that has about one quarter of our business.

I tried to work things out from a legal as well as moral standpoint, and came to the conclusion that we could give the discount provided we gave the same discount to all other customers who did the same volume of business.

There was a big hassle with the buyer for this chain because he wanted a particular kind of affidavit from me, specifying the discount on the first dollar's worth of business. It was a complicated situation, but at any rate I couldn't give the affidavit because to do so would have necessitated lying.

The buyer was perturbed. He told me he could produce an affidavit spelling everything out just the way he wanted it. I explained that if he could produce such an affidavit, he would be producing a lie. Then he said he didn't necessarily have to stand behind this affidavit, but he wanted to have it nevertheless.

At this point I could do no more than tell him that we would both end up as parties to a lie. Then I had to add that I had become a Christian, and to me if Christianity meant anything it had to mean everything. I couldn't go on claiming to be a Christian while living a lie just for the sake of business.

This was tough language for me to use on a customer, but I had to do it. He turned to me and said, "Patton, I could have you thrown out of here for that—and all your business with you." He got up, livid with rage, and walked away.

All I could do was sit there and pray, "Lord, You got me into this, and You know what the right answer is. I have to stand by my guns. So whatever this customer decides, I'll accept it. Now please see me through this."

Finally the man came back and sat down, and this is what he said: "Patton, I want you to call me every Monday morning and tell me how much business my stores are doing with you. I'm going to see to it that we get this maximum discount, with or without the affidavit, and that's that."

Now, I don't say this means that every time I am confronted with a problem, and stand up and do what I feel is right, God is going to answer it in such a dramatic fashion. Nor do I suppose He is always going to give me financial success. I think there will be times when He will ask me to do things that could very easily mean the end of my business. The question is, if that comes, what will I do?

As I write this, we are going through a financial crisis. My secretary-treasurer is very much worried. He says we don't have the money to pay our bills, and asks what we are going to do.

All I can say is this: I am going to make every reasonable effort to collect what is owed us; I am going to do as good a selling job as possible; but most of all I am going to pray.

My prayer is not, "Lord bring in all this money and let us get rich," but rather, "Lord, You do with this company what You want done."

People say to me, "Oh, it's all very well for you to talk about the Christian life—but what would you do if adversity came? If your business were taken away from you? Would you still believe?"

I know I could lose the company and all that goes with it, and people would probably say, "Well, Patton, this Christianity really caught up with you, didn't it?"

I know also that I would still be able to say that my Lord is Lord of all, and that I will serve Him come what may.

—*May, 1961*

I'll never forget the time one summer when Frank Patton bought an old bus and transported a whole bunch of teen-agers from Virginia to a camp in the Rocky Mountains. This is typical of the good-hearted, youthful things Frank has been up to since he became a Christian—things some people would regard as quixotic. I like Frank for it! He'd be the first to admit that his life is not "a piece of cake," that he still has problems and tensions. But I'm glad there are people like him in the world— people who add a touch of daring, a touch of gaiety, to an existence that all too often seems grimly gray.

Chapter 20

■

THE FIVE CHRISTS I HAVE KNOWN

by Leonard E. LeSourd
Executive Editor, "Guideposts"

If I have any one dominant and overwhelming conviction, it is that whenever or however we make it, the most important decision we ever make in our life concerns our relationship to Jesus Christ. Even if we never do anything at all about Him, this in itself constitutes a crucial decision.

My relationship to Christ has gone through four definite stages and is now in a fifth. The first stage was a negative one. It was my contact as a child with *the pale, anemic Jesus pictured on the Sunday school wall.* I encountered there a completely unimpressive image—"Gentle Jesus, meek and mild." Many have had a similar experience.

This is not an indictment of Sunday school teachers, for I know how difficult it is to capture the imagination of youth. Part of the problem involves the pictures and reading material in Sunday school publications. Few of these periodicals attempt to show Christ as masculine. To boys whose heroes are athletes, this is a very negative portrait of the Saviour of mankind. The result was that from my boyhood until I was almost twenty-seven years old, Jesus never seemed important to me. I believed in God, went to church, was a perfunctory Christian, but hardly ever gave a thought to Christ.

The second stage of my relationship to Christ developed in college. In this intellectual atmosphere there emerged *the histori-cal Christ*. Here is a comfortable position. The historical Jesus is usually set far back from the stream of life. With this approach, one is unlikely to be shunned or considered a fanatic for his beliefs. He can join the intellectual chorus and recite the words: "Jesus was a good man. He had some good advice for us, but let's be realistic about those myths and fairy tales you read about Him in the Bible. That stuff is completely unscientific."

The point, of course, is that any person who adopts this warped concept of Jesus is only a step away from the position of saying, "All religions are about the same." How much better if there were clear acceptance—or rejection, for what Jesus said about His divinity is so startling and to the point that if we *are* being realistic we either have to believe Him or consider Him a maniac.

In my case, putting Christ in this historical setting was a simple solution during college and four years as an Army Air Corps pilot. The historical Christ did not interfere with anything I wanted to do. My ego could rule supreme.

Yet when I faced up to the cold, clammy fear of death during World War II, I desperately needed a philosophy. With Christ so remote I had to find something. The result was an attitude of nonchalance—"It's not important whether you live or die." This "so what" attitude became my philosophy during those war years.

My drift from this "historical" relationship with Christ to a third stage—*Christ the Teacher*—began in 1946. I had been out of the Air Corps for about a year, wandering aimlessly around the country collecting material to write a novel. This project was a complete flop. My philosophy of nonchalance left me totally unadjusted to face the competition and realities of the postwar world.

When I returned home from my wanderings, my father, concerned about my aimlessness, suggested that I apply for a writing position with a small new religious publication called "Guideposts." I was not at all interested in religion, nor was I a very promising subject for such a job. Yet through an unusual chain of circumstances I found myself being interviewed by Dr. Norman Vincent Peale, founder of "Guideposts." He challenged me by saying, "There is a real need for a publication which can relate religious truths to the practical, down-to-earth problems facing people today. We need Christ's wisdom, and 'Guideposts' will bring it to readers through the story technique."

I accepted the job as a writer. Then spiritual development began for me as I interviewed people who had at the core of their lives a solid faith. I began to want what they had.

"Christ is the greatest teacher," a businessman told me one day, "and there is practical truth in the gospel for us today." Thus I began to see Christ in a new light. What He said two thousand years ago would be applied to me now. Take His words, "Ask and it shall be given you; seek and ye shall find; knock and it shall be opened unto you." Here was helpful advice in dreaming big dreams and accomplishing them. I was also intrigued by the passage, "I can do all things through Christ which strengtheneth me." What better guide to personal achievement?

Christ the Teacher emerged for me as a Man with a practical philosophy. He was a good psychologist. He knew people. He had something I could use. The phrase *spiritual technique* entered my vocabulary. All this meant that I was interested in Christ *not for what He was and is,* but for what He could do for me. I wanted to use Him for personal gain.

It took a church fellowship group to help me advance into the fourth stage—where I encountered *Christ the Person.* I walked into the Young Adult Group of Marble Collegiate Church one night in 1947. I was twenty-eight years old, cynical, and opinionated. I had cloaked myself with a pseudo-sophistication to cover up my basic loneliness and insecurity.

As I entered the door, I told myself that these church group meetings were a waste of time—just stuffy people talking about a vague Christianity. The strongest motivation for my going was the hope of finding a nice-looking date.

To my surprise I found attractive, intelligent people who displayed a genuine friendliness. Before I knew what had happened, I was pulled into some of their activities. Here were people who very obviously found Christ to be more than a teacher. Through them and through books, particularly *The Man Nobody Knows,* by Bruce Barton, my concept of a pale, meek, and mild Jesus was erased. The picture of a virile man with rippling muscles replaced the soft figure in my mind. I began to see the adventure of Christianity. I began to get a glimpse of how the Disciples must have felt following such a Man.

Soon I was invited to attend a weekend retreat with some of these young adults. I didn't fully understand the purpose of a retreat; in fact I disliked the word because it seemed to indicate a backward movement. Yet I found myself drawn to these particular people, their enthusiasm—and something more.

This particular weekend combined a series of discussions, periods of quiet meditation, and recreation. I loved the recreation, was bored during the meditation, and uncomfortable at the tone of the discussion in the meetings. The theme was on the importance of making a personal commitment to Jesus Christ.

At first I decided that I had already done this. After all, I *was* a member of the church. Soon I began to realize, however, that this was not what they were talking about. Like many, I had joined the church automatically, following the traditions of our family heritage. But what the members of this retreat group were talking about was a specific personal step beyond church membership.

When one of the members described how he had gone into a small chapel in one of the retreat buildings, knelt at the altar, and made this type of commitment, I found myself becoming more and more uneasy. This was an emotional aspect of religion that I had always avoided. I was afraid of it. It was a threat to my self-control—to the veneer of sophistication which had been carefully built up over the past years. Yet, I felt drawn to a quality of life I was seeing. My thoughts were turbulent, and underneath was emerging a sense of excitement. After the meeting, I found myself in the back of the same chapel. "What are you doing here?" I asked myself.

An unknown force was pulling me toward the altar; another holding me back. I had always hated the idea of any kind of surrender; I had always recoiled from kneeling. Yet here in this chapel I was suddenly challenged to do all these acts I had so studiously avoided in the past.

Slowly my legs carried me forward down the aisle to the altar. There was a last-minute stiffened resistance. Then slowly, easily, my knees bent. I found myself saying a very simple prayer— *"Lord Jesus, I don't really know how I happen to be here, but I feel that I want to surrender my life to you. I do so now. Show me what I am to do next."*

Immediately there was a great sense of release, joy, exhilaration. I felt a kind of cleansing, a revitalization.

This experience climaxed my growing relationship to Christ the Person. It was a confrontation that was to affect every area of my life—habits, thoughts, work, play, family.

The years immediately afterwards were rich and full. I had a new enthusiasm for my job and for Christ. Marriage followed and three children were born in seven years. "Guideposts" grew and expanded—eventually reaching a circulation of one million.

In the middle 1950's we moved away from New York City, away from the close fellowship of the Marble Collegiate group.

Looking back now I can see that I never wavered too far from my feelings of closeness to Christ, but I did have trouble seeking His will as against my own.

Then came calamity—a divorce; with it, disruption of family life, emotional upset and frustration. Much of the problem involved circumstances over which I had no control. Yet I kept asking myself over and over again, *Why had it happened?* I had surrendered my life to Christ. I had worked hard at being a good Christian. Somehow I felt that commitment to Christ guaranteed a life free of major disasters like this.

The spiritual decline came quickly. Discouragement and confusion are great tools of the devil. But one rock I had to hold on to was that act of surrender to Christ. When my decline reached a desperate and crucial point, once again I got down on my knees and re-committed my life to Christ. It was another beginning.

There was a difference this time from before. Now I recognized my frailty, my human weaknesses. I knew that it was not enough to have Christ just as a Leader, or a Guide, or a nearby Presence. *I had to have His Spirit within me.* It was then that I became really aware that there was an Indwelling Christ. This is the stage I am now in—learning, exploring, trying to grow.

It is so perfectly illustrated by the story of the Disciples. Humble men, dedicated, they all committed their lives to their Master. They thought that they had done all that was necessary, yet the commitment was not enough. When trouble came, all faltered: Judas betrayed Christ, Peter denied Him, the rest fled in panic when Jesus was apprehended and crucified.

Yet the great miracle of Christianity is what happened to these confused and inadequate men at Pentecost. Christ appeared to them and said, "You shall receive power when the Holy Spirit has come upon you."

The Disciples gathered in the Upper Room and prayed deeply

for many hours. The Bible describes the "rush of mighty wind" that came, and how "they were all filled with the Holy Spirit." What a sight this must have been! How indescribable the joy, the elation, the resurgence of power as these men were reborn. The Holy Spirit filled them all with such power that they were able to go forth and bring Christianity to the world in spite of threats, ridicule, and apathy—in spite of beatings, imprisonment, and execution.

The Holy Spirit was indeed within these Disciples. There is no other explanation for all that they accomplished.

I see now that this Indwelling Christ is what I need. For it is through His Spirit that Christ can change people, revitalize them. and send them forth to win the world. I want to be part of such a movement! *—April, 1963*

The success of "Guideposts" is one of the publishing phenomena of our time. From slender beginnings, it has grown to staggering dimensions. Len LeSourd is intimately associated with its amazing development, and the fact that he was willing to find time to write his own story for FAITH AT WORK surprises me to this day, and increases my admiration for Len as an editor and as a man. What makes Len's narrative so useful is that it chronicles very skillfully one man's spiritual development, providing hope and insight for every reader who finds himself in one of the stages described in the story. Moreover, the author is careful to point out that his story is unfinished. This is a characteristic of every honest spiritual odyssey.

PART THREE

■

ANSWERING
THE WORLD'S ANGUISH

The world's needs are overwhelming—its demands unending.
For those living the great adventure, fulfillment lies not in retreat
but in service. In the business world . . . the home . . . the
school . . . in politics and poverty . . . in pain and prison . . .
in slums and in "high society" they hear the eternal voice say,
"Who will go?" And they answer, "Here am I; send me."

The way is neither simple nor easy, but it promises—and
provides—life infinitely worth living.

Chapter 21

■

A COUNTER FOR ENCOUNTER

Bill Iverson's Story

It was Friday morning. In his study at the First Reformed Church, Newark, New Jersey, Bill Iverson was putting the finishing touches on his Sunday sermon. From Jesus' words to Peter, "Launch out into the deep and let down your nets," he intended to challenge his people to "get out where the fish are," and bear witness for Christ.

The sermon was a good one, so good that it began to speak back to Bill as he prepared it, and call to mind his own frustrations in witnessing. For seven years in this inner-city parish he had been concerned for the drunks, the down-and-outers, and especially the teen-agers who did not come to church, and the barrier his ministerial role seemed to impose on him.

At AA meetings he had watched the defenses of entrenched alcoholics drop when they listened to one another, and he saw their willingness to share their problems. But alcoholics didn't talk to preachers that freely. Nor did teen-agers. Either they were hostile to clergymen or they put them so high on a pedestal that they couldn't reveal their true feelings. How could it be made easier for them to do so?

Bill thought back to an open-air meeting he had once held near West Side High School and the picture of a luncheonette on the corner flashed into his mind—an ideal spot to reach teen-

145

agers. He chuckled as he thought of how his Sunday morning text might read, "*Lunch* out into the deep."

That afternoon he drove by West Side High School and there, across from the school, was the luncheonette with a big red sign in the window, "For Sale." Bill went in, told the owner what he had in mind, and asked if he could hire on for a day to get the feel of things. The place was teeming with kids. The juke box was jumping to the beat of the Beatles and the smoke was like a London fog. On Tuesday Bill bought it.

Now he had a counter instead of a pulpit and it allowed for two-way conversations. Young people talked freely to him about school, about their parents, about sex and dope. Even after they discovered that Bill was an ordained minister it made no difference. He had identified with them by buying the luncheonette, he was willing to listen to them, and they trusted him. In seven months he made more friends among teen-agers than he had in the seven years previously.

But how could Bill make the encounters over the counter most meaningful? He began to develop a questionnaire, which evolved finally into twenty questions, and which he now keeps on a clipboard on the wall. When business is slow and a boy or girl is lounging at the counter Bill may take down the clipboard and ask for an interview.

What do you think of young people today? Is the world getting better or worse? Does life have a purpose? Do you believe in God? Is God interested in you personally? So go the questions. And the teen-ager is flattered to be asked his opinions, often interrupting to ask, "Did you get that straight?" as Bill carefully records each answer.

A teen-age girl is sitting at the counter, sipping a Coke and daydreaming. When Bill asks for an interview she says, "Sure." She is serious in her answers. God is not interested in her personally. (Because grown-ups aren't, perhaps?) The world is getting worse. (She lives over the tavern where her father works; her mother drinks too much; and mother and father have never married.) *Did Jesus Christ rise from the dead?* She says Yes, recalling a church background. *For what purpose?* She doesn't know. The interview ends as Bill gives her a little book (for the "incubation period," he says), and she promises to read it and talk to him again.

Two weeks later she is again alone at the counter. She has read the book and has been thinking. "You said God isn't personal," Bill begins; "but if Jesus Christ is alive He can live in you." "That's what I want," she responds, and there at the counter she bows her head and asks the Lord to come into her life. Her first act as a new Christian is to bring in a girl friend, and she too turns her life over to Christ at the counter. A Negro boy, overhearing the conversation, says, "Bill, I'll be back seventh period," and he too commits himself to Jesus Christ.

Interviewing is a time-honored way to encourage personal encounter. It is a way of saying to people, "What you think is important," and it may open the door to deep understanding of what a person thinks and feels.

Soon Bill was in over his head. The luncheonette seemed an ideal place for occasional meetings on Friday nights. A weekend retreat in the mountains could telescope the influence of weeks and months into a few hours. There were parents to meet and counsel. Besides all this there was the doctoral dissertation on "adolescent attitudes" crying to be written so that Bill could finish his work at New York University. So in September, 1964, he resigned his pastorate.

But with his salary gone Bill couldn't make ends meet. He was losing money on the luncheonette and in January he was forced to close down. Earl Triplett, the safety officer on the corner, almost wept that day. And the kids were bewildered. They had come to count on Bill's always being there.

Bill's friends felt he must reopen, especially one big fellow whom he had led to Christ and who offered to help out behind the counter without pay. Others joined him, and in March signs in the windows announced happily, "Bill's back."

How long will Bill be on that corner cooking hamburgers and talking to teen-agers? He doesn't know. He feels he's experimenting in new ways to communicate the gospel. Perhaps other Christians will join him and open luncheonettes at other strategic locations in Newark. But first of all the first luncheonette must pay its way. Meanwhile the principles he is learning can apply anywhere—to a parent in his relations with his children, or to a Sunday school teacher or youth worker in a church. "If you can have a heart-to-heart talk with a teen-ager," Bill says, "be honest with him, and get him to be honest with you, God can use you."

When Bill talks to youth workers in the churches, as he frequently does, he is likely to share with them some recent professional findings about would-be teen-age suicides in New Jersey. It has been found that teen-agers want strong adult authority figures and adults who will listen to them, as well as acceptance by their own peer group.

They are crying for adults whom they can respect and who will tell them what to do at the right time. Their attitude may seem to say, "Don't tell us anything," but they are actually asking that we earn the right to speak, and when we do they want to hear what we have to say. They can spot a phony. Perhaps that's why so many adults shy away from teen-age involvement. (Who wants to be exposed?) But teen-agers aren't asking for perfection—just honesty and integrity—what any adult ought to be able to give.

Bill believes that the supreme authority every young person wants, whether he knows it or not, is Jesus Christ, but to discover this fact he must see His Lordship mirrored in the lives of people. The person who knows how to listen will get his chance to speak. This world, with its television and radio and fast-paced living, militates against two people sitting down and having honest conversation, but we've got to find the time and occasion for it and we've got to *want* to listen. The threat of what we might hear, of what we might see in ourselves, and of how little we might have to offer is our greatest barrier. But here the Christian gospel is most helpful. If we are discovering ourselves in God's love we don't need to pretend to be more than we are, to defend ourselves, or to fear exposure.

When God exposes a human being He does it through another human being. Bill insists that his own exposure and growth has occurred not so much from being alone in prayer and with the Bible as from being "in dialogue" with other honest and dedicated people. Perhaps all of us have had the experience of becoming a little bit honest and have seen the person we were talking to respond even more honestly, until soon both of us have dropped all barriers and are talking heart to heart. In the encounter both people are changed.

If we want to talk to teen-agers we must drop our facades and let our phoniness go. This is a growing process, to be sure, but it is only in terms of our own honesty that teen-agers can see themselves. If we're not real they can't be real, and will grow up imitating the phony world—either inside or outside of the Church—and missing the greatest experience life can offer, the encounter with reality which is God Himself. —*May, 1965*

Publicity can be helpful. Articles in FAITH AT WORK, "Guideposts," and other magazines brought Bill Iverson allies in his struggle to keep the "counter for encounter" in operation. It is not easy sledding, of course, and whether Bill will be in business when you read this is an open question. Nevertheless, his pioneering has marked a trail for those who are eager to

meet teen-agers where they live and help them in ways they will
accept. One of the continuing marvels of Christianity is the ap-
pearance of new ideas and movements that thrive awhile, fade,
but yield a rich harvest. Does it remind you of the story of the
grain of wheat that fell into the ground . . . ?

Chapter 22

HOW TO PASS ON YOUR FAITH

by Mary Brinig
Housewife, Gilmanton, New Hampshire;
Former Director of Activities at Marble Collegiate Church,
New York City

The most exciting experiences in life are the extraordinary
transformations in people and situations that Christ brings
through ordinary persons who seek and find His redemptive plan
for their lives. Needy people are everywhere, some defeated by
sin and failure, others wasted and wistful for a dynamic purpose
in life. Christ is constantly giving us opportunities to demonstrate
and communicate His love to them.

But first, we must know these in our own experience and be
able to tell specifically and effectively just what He has done
for us. Years ago, like many a "good Christian" I went about
doing good with much emphasis on the "going about." I taught
a Sunday school class and served as a parole officer in court
trying to rehabilitate morally defeated women and girls.

One day a prostitute said to me, "I don't want to go on this
way, but I have no power over temptation. You believe in God;
how do you get His power into your life to do something you
can't do alone?" I had nothing to say to her. Although Christ
meant much to me in general, He seemed to mean little in
particular. I could think of nothing specific that seemed relevant

151

to her need or to my own. This shocked me into a search for reality which came in a commitment to God's *will*, not just to His work. Since then I have sought His will for all my relationships—family, neighbors, and acquaintances—and have developed a sense of adventuring with God, even in a routine meeting, a party, or a casual encounter in a supermarket.

We can miss the daily opportunities for communicating our faith, and the amazing chain reaction that they often set in motion, if we are not alert. I try to keep in mind four things.

Any expression of a personal need or frustration is an obvious chance to tell how God has helped us in a similar situation. If there is no time to share deeply, we can say, "That's the kind of thing I've learned to pray about and I've found it makes a great difference in my ability to cope with it," or "I'll be praying about it for you." This gives us the opportunity to bring up the subject at a later time when we can go into the matter more fully.

When someone is critical or gossipy or negative about a person or situation, we can say, "How do you think we (or you) might help?" Then we can say how we have been led to help in similar situations, or to understand why people do what they do, and thereby find our criticism changing to compassion or constructive helpfulness. I discovered that jealousy was at the root of my criticism of one person and, in admitting this, I have helped others to face their own attitudes honestly.

An opportunity is frequently presented in discussions of world or community problems. The realization that we are all part of the problem and must begin with ourselves in order to change the world can lead to a sharing of any convictions or experiences that could make us part of the answer.

I report spiritual experiences to friends as excitedly as I would any other enthusiasm. Sometimes this leads to further conversations with people who normally think of religion as deadly dull. I did this one time with a former school classmate, a delightful pagan. We had rarely met since college days, when neither of us was the least bit interested in religion. As we were catching up on the intervening years, I told her glowingly of my discovery of a new purpose in life. She was so captivated that she asked me to tell my story to her bridge group who were coming for the afternoon.

Early in the game we both heard someone at another table say, "No one is interested in religion any more as an answer to anything." My friend spoke up loudly, "Mary is! Mary, tell them some of the things you were just telling me." I was a bit scared, but I sent up an S.O.S. to God to help me say the right things, and began. We didn't play any more bridge. Everyone began to mention needs and ask questions, and as a result, a lot happened, both to my friend and to some of her friends in the days that followed.

There are casual encounters in which we too often fail because the person involved does not seem as important to us as was the woman at the well to Jesus. While walking up Fifth Avenue one day, I encountered a scenario writer whom I had met in a hotel a few weeks before. She had just come from a discouraging interview and was thinking of returning to Hollywood. I suggested a cup of coffee to indicate my interest in her and drew out her story, listening more than I talked. Her Broadway-Hollywood background was very different from mine. She had been married and divorced three times, was presently supported by another man, was rooming with a night-club entertainer, and seemed to me sophisticated, jaded, disillusioned.

I would have been shocked had I not come to the deep conviction that all sin is equally black to God, and my need for forgiveness for my more "respectable" sins of insincerity and prejudice was just as great as hers. Therefore, I could neither criticize nor condemn her, but neither did I know what to say.

As she talked, I prayed that God would tell me how to share

my faith intriguingly and in terminology that she would understand. I found myself saying, "I believe God has a wonderful plan for each person's life. He has given you some great talents for writing and He wants to use you and help you find fulfillment." She was stunned and asked me why I believed that. I related the bit of my own experience that seemed relevant. She looked as though I were talking Greek, shrugged, and said, "I wish I could believe it," and prepared to leave. I suggested that she call on me if she ever wanted to talk more about it, and gave her my address. We parted with my promise to pray about her situation. I always try to leave the door ajar for further opportunities.

Often God uses us with a person for the first step or two, and then He moves him on to other influences when he is ready. Others we may help to a decision after many months. We must trust all of this to Him. However, the scenario writer called in three days and asked to come over for a talk. Before she arrived, I had a time of prayer and listening to God about the interview. Three important guidelines came to mind which have been valuable since in similar situations:

1. Do not tell her what to do but only what you have done and what has happened. Share your own struggle.

2. Help her to spill out her whole story without interruption. Don't assume anything or leap to conclusions. You might treat only the symptoms and not the disease.

3. Help her to pinpoint her real need, make a moral inventory, and get her own insight about the next step she should take.

After an hour of talking, I suggested that we have a quiet time and explained to her what it involved. I said I would pray that God would show her where to begin, what changes would have to be made in order to find His plan for her. We were quiet for a few minutes before I heard her writing. Eight things had come to her mind that needed to be changed or given up, including the man who was supporting her. But heading her list was "drinking." When I asked why that was first, since it seemed comparatively unimportant, she said, "If I take a drink, I will not keep my decisions about the other things. It is basic to any real change." That taught me never to minimize another person's conviction of sin.

I invited her to climax her decision by committing her life— and each of these specific things—to God aloud in prayer. I told her of my own acceptance of God's forgiveness and how I found His power for new creative living through a daily time of prayer, seeking guidance, and devotional reading. I suggested that we meet regularly for deep sharing of temptations and problems and growth.

The results with this new friend were fantastic. She became a leader in a Christian group full of show people in New York and later in a similar group in Hollywood. Through her the man in her life was dramatically changed. He made restitution to his ex-wife and son who said that for seventeen years he had hated his father and never wanted to meet him, but now he wanted to commit his own life to the God who had so changed his father. Subsequently, the son was baptized in our church. The woman shared her decision with her third ex-husband, a famous auto racer and stunt driver in the movies. His life was changed. The life-changing influence from this one changed life went on and on.

When we give our lives to God to use in His redemptive plan for the world, He not only releases a far-reaching chain reaction, but our lives find the exciting purpose and the highest fulfillment for which He created us. —*January, 1966*

Mary and Harold Brinig have earned a well-deserved retirement in a sleepy New England village, but it hasn't seemed to slow them down very much. Their tremendous vitality and wide experience are still available to people in all kinds of ways. The phenomenal Young Adults organization they built at Marble Collegiate Church has been influential in changing the lives of many hundreds of young people, and stands as an enduring monument to their faith and leadership. Harold, with his gruff charm; Mary, with her grace and brilliance—they are unforgettable. With them I have shared plans in a conference room, prayer in a speeding car, a picnic supper on the beach, all adding up to a total impression of love that will remain with me forever.

Chapter 23

■

ANSWER FOR ANN

by J. J. Lamberts
Professor of English, Tempe, Arizona

I will call the young lady Ann. A colleague of mine had been trying to fill a summer job and she seemed a promising candidate. I invited Ann to have coffee with me at the coffee shop where I explained what the position involved and why I considered her qualifications sufficient. That taken care of, I asked a few questions about her education, her family, and similar matters. For no reason that I can call to mind I inquired whether she was associated with any church.

"I used to be a Catholic," she said, "but now I guess I'm nothing."

"How'd that happen?"

"Oh, I always kept getting into arguments with the nuns. I'd ask questions and they'd tell me I was just supposed to be quiet and believe. They kicked me out of class a couple of times and the third time they kicked me out I stayed away."

"And then what?"

"Well, I guess I don't believe in God or anything else very much."

"Oh."

"Is that bad?"

"Is what bad, Ann?"

157

"Not believing God."

"Why, no. You certainly can't be honest with yourself and not doubt Him at some time in your life."

"I'm glad to hear that."

"Just the same, He does exist. What's more, He is taking a very real interest in you."

"I'm not so sure."

"The fact of the matter is that He's ready to accept you as you are. All you have to be willing to do is accept His acceptance."

"I can't do that. I don't even believe He exists."

"I wouldn't expect you to be able to. Certainly not here and now."

For maybe five, maybe ten, more minutes we talked. It was time to leave.

"Ann," I said, "would you mind if I did one thing?"

"What's that?"

"I'm going to start praying for you."

For a moment Ann looked bewildered. Then she brightened and said, "If anyone had told me that an hour ago I'd have said he was crazy. Now I appreciate it very much."

Ann used to stop and visit me during the next few weeks and we talked about various things, sometimes about her courses, sometimes her experiences, sometimes her beliefs and doubts. One day I told her:

"Young lady, before long you're going to make a decision about all this."

"I think maybe I will," she said.

A short while afterwards—a week or two—we were in conversation again and this time I realized that she had definitely taken hold of something, or perhaps it was that Someone had taken hold of her. She seemed more eager to fight the matter out. Still she had no intention of giving up easily and she offered one argument after another; each, it seemed, a little weaker than the one before.

"I wish I could be sure of these things," she said. "You're a scholar yourself and you know how these old manuscripts were put together. We can't be expected to read a book like the Bible and blindly believe everything it says, can we?"

"I'll grant you that."

"Well, then, what is it?"

"All I've been trying to tell you is this. As human beings we are obliged to have something at the center of our lives. It may be an ambition or some person we greatly admire. Usually it's ourselves. We're sure that we can run our lives adequately, but things have a way of caving in on us just often enough to remind us that a human life is more than one person can handle. You see, Ann, God makes us an offer that He will take over the direction of our lives. It's your will—your ability to tell God 'yes' or 'no'—that stands between you and Him. It's terribly simple and yet terribly complicated."

"I think I see what you mean."

"What we have to do—each one of us—is to turn over our wills to God and let Him be at the center of our lives."

"How can I do that when I'm not even sure He exists?"

"That's the problem. You don't know He exists, but you have to believe it. You simply let go, by an act of complete believing, and when you've done that you'll find a miracle has happened. There will be another you."

"Is there any proof for that?"

"Why, sure, it's happened to thousands of people—Paul, for instance, and . . ."

"Oh, you can't tell me that!" she interrupted hotly. "All we've got is the books again. We don't know what really went on."

"Then would you let me tell you what happened to me? You see, I always supposed I was a perfectly adequate person . . ."

And so I told her my entire story, simply and honestly. I wanted her to realize that there was indeed a difference, that there had been such a thing as a "before and after." She listened quietly till the end of the story.

"I believe you're right," she said. "I want that too."

"Then would you mind if I prayed now, Ann?"

"Oh, no. Would you?"

"Dear God," I said, "here's Ann. You've always known her, and I know you've loved her much more than she can imagine being loved. She isn't going to bring you anything except herself. Will you give her the courage now to let go and to find herself in the Everlasting Arms?"

Then to Ann I said, "Now you tell Him."

"Why, He's right here in the room with us," she said. "Yes, God. Here I am."

There was a silence and then a little gasp from Ann.

"Something's happened. All of a sudden I'm quite different. Oh . . ."

So here was Ann, at once and rather unexpectedly become a believer. Perhaps if I had not gone through the narrow gate myself, and if I had not found myself required to relinquish all of my beloved rules and cherished conditions outside the wall, I should have been pretty doubtful that anything could come of this. For poor Ann was simply a mass of raw places where she had been bruised by organized religion and by "good" people. It wasn't only the Roman Catholic Church, but there had been— and still was—a churchgoing, text-quoting roommate who knew everything but the mercy of the Lord.

In the drawer of my desk was a pocket New Testament. I took the book out of the drawer and handed it to her.

"I don't suppose you have a Bible, do you? Let me give you this."

"Thank you." She began looking at it with a new eagerness.

"You'll want to find out about the Person who's begun running your life, and I think one of these days you'll get to know Him as Jesus Christ."

"That doesn't mean anything to me yet."

"I'm not surprised. It all takes time. But be sure to read this."

"What are these?" She began reading through the index, "Matthew, Mark, Luke . . ."

"Those are just the life of Jesus Christ as several different people told it. There are four of them. The next section is called Acts and it's the story of the first believers."

"And then what are the rest of these?"

"Mostly letters that men like Paul and Peter wrote to various groups of early Christians."

"Oh, I see. Biography and history and correspondence. How neat."

"What did you expect?"

"I don't know. A kind of rule book, I guess, to tell me what I could do and what I couldn't"

I had never realized how little God needs in order for Him to start making over a life. Even the word "God" jarred this girl, and "Jesus Christ" was equally disturbing. She wondered whether He would have any objections if she called Him "Supreme Being" until she got better acquainted. I was sure He wouldn't. A few days later she discovered that she was able to love other people— most particularly those who had irritated her before. Three weeks were scarcely past when I heard her telling her unbelieving sister she "had become a Christian." I had supposed it would take Ann longer than three weeks to get used to thinking of herself as a Christian. But, just in that brief time, the miracle had happened.

—October, 1960

Jack and Louise Lamberts have an unusual gift for dialogue with people who are looking for answers to life's complex ques-

tions. This gift is demonstrated perhaps most clearly by their encounters with youngsters—the cynical, the lost, the despairing, the sensation-seeking. You'd think to make these kinds of contacts they'd have to be "swingers" themselves—and perhaps they are! But when you meet Louise, your first impression is of a pretty but quite conventional housewife. Jack seems the classic scholar—a bit dry, laconic, with a sense of humor that demands sharp ears and considerable erudition on the part of his friends. The Lamberts are marvelously effective people, good companions, and trail-blazers in lay renewal.

Chapter 24

THE DOOR GOD LEFT OPEN

by Mary Helen Beale
Rest Home Proprietor, Montgomery, Alabama

Merry Wood Lodge, nestled in a wooded area twenty-five miles north of our home in Montgomery, Alabama, is a twenty-four bed nursing home for the aged, convalescent, and chronically ill. As I drive there each morning, I come to a rise in the highway that overlooks hazy blue hills in the distance.

Each time I reach this view there flashes through my mind, "I will lift up mine eyes unto the hills from whence cometh my help; my help cometh from the Lord who made heaven and earth."

From that point on, for the next few miles, the Lord and I talk about the day to come at Merry Wood. He renews His promise to be with us through any circumstance that arises and I claim His promise. For the Lord gave my husband Coleman and me this ministry to the sick and aging in a very special way.

Coleman spent thirty years in the world of finance and insurance, and in the course of those years founded two companies which are still operating successfully. He was competent and modestly successful, but when he was fifty, unpleasant circumstances necessitated his leaving the business. For two years he explored possibilities for new ventures. Each new idea seemed good and we would get almost to the point of thinking "this is it" when, for reasons we couldn't understand, the door would slam. Discouragement, doubts, and fears moved in to live with us—and they aren't good house guests.

From a worldly point of view there was a reason for our anxiety. Two of our children were of college age and the third wasn't far behind. We were in the most financially demanding time of our lives.

In October, 1962, Louise and Sidney Mohr, two dynamic Christians from Montgomery, spearheaded the first Faith at Work conference held in the Southeast at Camp Grandview in our area. We love Louise and Sid dearly, so we went—not reluctantly, but cautiously.

Coleman wasn't at all sure that God could be present in such informal surroundings. His God lived primarily in the ritual of the Episcopal Church, of which he is now a communicant, or in the mass of the Roman Church, in which he had been brought up. The God he knew didn't come close to common problems. As for me, I took dim view of the word "fellowship" and was offended at the "praying togetherness" of the people at the conference.

At the opening session, Don James witnessed. We didn't know he was a minister. He certainly didn't look like one to us as he sat on the edge of the table, swinging one foot and telling of his first prayer group experiences as an insurance salesman after World War II. But we both loved him. We felt he was genuine, honest, dynamic, human, and Christian, and we listened.

Coleman was in Don's "talk-it-over" group. When the group members began to say, "God said this to me," Coleman told the truth as he knew it, "I'm sorry, but God's never opened His mouth to me." Don countered with, "Do you want Him to speak to you?" Then and there the group prayed for Coleman, and for the first time in his life Coleman prayed aloud.

As for me, I was pretty insufferable. I had read for many

years from the writings of C. S. Lewis, J. B. Phillips, Sam Shoemaker, Reuel Howe, Elton Trueblood, and many others. Mine
was the intellectual approach, and I was smug in thinking I
knew the answers. In spite of warnings that one can't go the
Christian way alone, I still didn't accept the need for fellowship.
I considered myself a reserved Christian—a bit too dignified for
such open talk. But I was sitting in a group led by Chaplain
Conway Lanford of Maxwell Air Force Base. Con must have
some Quaker in his background, for he believes in long silences
as well as in speaking out. There were deep stirrings within me.

On the second night of the conference, Don and Coleman
disappeared. They went "off to the woods" for man-to-man con-
fessions and for Coleman to pour out his fears and anxieties.
Later I learned they had agreed to pray for thirty days concern-
ing Coleman's next business move.

All I needed for the "leap of faith" was my husband's hand
in mine, and, by Sunday morning, no words were needed for us
to know that we would take the leap together. We knew we were
committed to as much as we understood. We surrendered, but
just how much we didn't really know.

The next few weeks found the new Coleman trying to take
the Kingdom by storm and getting spiritual indigestion. He would
recover, read, and pray some more. The crowning event for the
final seal of surrender was a men's retreat held at Hayesville,
North Carolina, by the men's prayer groups of the Chattahoo-
chee Valley in Georgia. On that mountaintop this new Christian
had a mountaintop experience.

An incident that occurred a few months before is probably the
key to our story. The preceding summer, while renewing my
teacher's certificate at our local college, I met a wonderful Christian, Mary Stuart Mims, who at the age of thirty had started as
a freshman in college with the avowed goal of earning an M.D.
degree so that she might be a medical missionary. Mary casually

mentioned one day that she owned a nursing home. I didn't know or care about nursing homes, but the Lord planted the chance remark in my mind to be used later.

As for Coleman's thirty-day-prayer experiment with Don, when three weeks had passed and there was not a break in our business dilemma, Coleman awoke one morning overcome by discouragement. Always full of wifely advice, I suggested that he not go downtown but work that morning in his woodworking shop, and, for the first time in my life, I read the want ads. There under Business Developments I read, "Nursing Home for sale within twenty-five miles of Montgomery." Something clicked. Quick as a flash, I called Mary Mims, brusquely asked the details and went flying to the workshop to say, "Come, Coleman, get your jacket. We are going to look at a nursing home and I think we are going to buy it."

During the ride, we were both sure that "this really was it" and we began to fight the Lord. Oh, how we did "fume and fuss." We told Him that we didn't want a nursing home and knew nothing about them. Coleman knew finance and I knew group work and teaching. How could the Lord do this to us? We said to ourselves that we refused to accept this as the answer, but we would look at it anyway.

At the home, we felt anything but loving. Here was illness, senility, mental retardation, and we felt waves of revulsion. Never, we said to ourselves, could we face this each day. How we laugh now. You see, we hadn't reckoned with the grace of God, with His mighty power to remove these unlovely and unloving feelings.

To say that the next few weeks were a struggle is a real understatement. We sought Christian and non-Christian advice from a very few friends, for we weren't ready for many people to know what we were considering. We found, to our surprise, that the nursing home business was an up and coming one. But Merry Wood was such a modest home and needed so much work.

Finally we dictated strongly to the Lord and told Him how He had slammed all those other doors. Now He could slam this one with the same mighty rush. The door stayed open and through it shone a golden light which beckoned our patients-to-be.

On January 1, 1963, we joined hands as partners with Mary Stuart Mims at Merry Wood Lodge. Legally speaking, I became the partner, but how could we get along at Merry Wood without our "Santa Claus Christian," Coleman?

What has happened in the last twelve months? The year has gone with lightning speed. Remodeling and expansion to a forty-bed home is under way after twelve frustrating months of getting our plans approved by the Alabama State Health Department. Our state standards, we are thankful to say, are rigorous. This makes for an upgrading of the entire nursing home business. We have tried to educate ourselves as quickly as possible by attending the state and national nursing home conventions and workshops, by subscribing to and reading professional magazines, by taking advantage of in-service training programs in our home, and by visiting other establishments. After all, we don't want to do a sloppy, unprofessional job for the Lord.

We are a skilled nursing home so we assume our obligation to give good nursing care first. But our minds whirl with other plans. There are picnics on the patio; Halloween parties; movies such as the "Life of a Patriot" from Williamsburg; Thanksgiving feasts; two weeks of Christmas festivities; Sunday afternoon parties for visitors; the *Merry Wood Ledger,* a monthly newspaper; ceramics classes; "talking books" from the Library of Congress for those with poor vision; and, most important of all, a daily afternoon Bible and Prayer group where we give thanks, intercede for our loved ones, and cast our burdens on the Lord.

What remains of our first feeling? Nothing. The Lord has stretched our hearts and sympathies by His grace until every patient has more than room there. His outpouring of love through us to them is one of His miracles. I like to think of Merry Wood as a tiny little piece of God's Kingdom, where there is a climate of acceptance for all, from our forty-nine-year-old "girl" with the mind of a five-year-old to our ninety-three-year-old "boy" who lives in the past. We all have some problems at Merry Wood, so no one is "different."

On my daily visit with each patient, I feel the "emotional pulse" and try to see that he or she is undergirded with the necessary love and assurance to meet his physical and mental trials. There are discouragements, of course, but all fade away when, as happened just before Christmas, one patient, who had hardly spoken for five years, managed a complete sentence: "I am ready for Santa Claus."

Lest you think this is a "pie in the sky," "live happily ever afterwards" witness, let me bring you back to earth. Of course we have cross words between patients, of course we have hurt feelings, of course we have grumbling. Certainly Coleman and I still have concerns. Merry Wood is not meeting all of our financial needs. Coleman still does not know whether he is to stay in the nursing home or whether it is just for me. Perhaps his mission, after this apprenticeship, is to establish a Christian business in the money market. *We do not know.*

I sometimes look longingly at my old life. I love gracious living—a brightly burning fire, polished silver tea services, and a relaxing afternoon cup of tea with my friends of this world. There is nothing wrong with this. There just isn't time right now. I feel fragmented, at times, between the home where my "blood family" lives and the home given me through the "blood of the Lamb." There is never enough time for either and I get satanically fearful that I will become physically bankrupt because I get so tired. "O ye of little faith!"

All we know is that, like Paul, we didn't really do any volunteering for the Lord. He just reached down and picked us up and put us where He wanted us. We try "not to doubt in the dark what we have been shown in the light."

We know, too, that even though our average age at Merry Wood is eighty, we aren't just sitting out the last years waiting to go to heaven. Neither are we "cramming for the finals." Instead, we are trying to bring a bit of heaven down to earth for the here and now. We just go merrily along planning for our future!   —*January, 1964*

The thought of old age and infirmity may strike terror to our hearts, especially if we envision the possibility of being left alone and unable to provide for ourselves. Therefore a story like Mary Helen Beale's, with all it implies of a well-balanced life for oldsters and the handicapped in homes like Merry Wood Lodge, can help to allay our fears and also indicate ways in which we can be of service to others.

Chapter 25

■

THE WAR WITHIN

by Lionel A. Whiston
Congregational Minister, Wrentham, Massachusetts

Outwardly I was a hard-working, successful pastor, conscientiously toiling for parishioners and community. Inwardly I was torn and frustrated. After ten years in a New England city church, I would come to the end of the day dissatisfied, wondering how many more calls I should have made that afternoon; angry because the plans I had presented at the evening meeting had been strongly opposed, and finally adopted in a woefully emasculated form; unhappy because last Sunday's sermon left much to be desired.

I was torn between loyalties to home and church, to family and parish. Appointments, conferences, and meetings kept me occupied night after night. Once when he was ten years old my son filled out and signed an information card from the church pew, checking the square opposite the line "desire a pastoral call!" My wife alternately complained of loneliness and showed me extra love because she saw my crowded program and sympathized with my tension and often-depleted spirit.

Deeper still was the heartache caused by the variance between my inner self and the image I presented to the world. And though the church—the institutional church—grew and prospered, very few people were significantly affected. After ten years of my ministry, the church officials seemed just as difficult to understand, and exhibited the same traits as when I had first come. And indeed, my own life had not changed.

"Lee, you remind me of what Jesus must have been like— always loving and caring for others," someone said, and it went to my heart like a dagger. I loved praise, but I knew how unworthy I was of such an estimation. There were areas of pride, ambition, lust, resentment in me that no one knew anything about. What had made me the kind of man I was?

My parents separated when I was ten years old. So uncommon and so disgraceful was a broken home in England in those days that my schoolmates jeered and threw stones and mud at me. I bore the hurt alone. Above all I longed for my father's love and approval, for I had chosen to live with him. I studied hard and brought home report cards that might have five A's and one B. "How is it that you got that B?" my father would say. He wanted to spur me on to perfection, but it was painful to me that I could never win his complete approval.

My constant striving for perfection was in time transferred from my father to God, and from my teens into my thirties I tried desperately to please my Heavenly Father by hard work and self-effort.

Courtship and marriage brought happiness, but I never really opened my heart to my wife, or to anyone else. Inwardly I was a coward, fearful of significant encounters. Instead, I kept up the pattern of trying to please people.

Because my thoughts were not verbalized, they turned inward and became daydreams that gave me satisfaction in times of frustration. I fancied myself the captain of a ball team, making the winning touchdown or hitting the grand slam home run. My romantic fantasies knew no bounds.

Civil war raged within me. I prayed for victory, only to fall periodically, especially after a time of exhausting service to others, such as after Christmas or Easter when I was spiritually depleted. Then I would turn to my fantasy world for relief, only to find myself more hopeless and unhappy than before.

I would kneel behind the pulpit as early as five o'clock on a Sunday morning, pleading with God to make me worthy to preach. Thus the struggle went on for a score of years, taking its toll and resulting in ulcers and four nervous breakdowns.

Eventually I reached the end of the road. I was desperately afraid that my thought patterns had permanently enslaved me. At my lowest moment I happened to be watching the tide flow into one of the inlets on the coast of Maine, and as I turned to God in prayer the thought flashed through my mind, "You poor fool, you are taking a pail, running to the point, filling it from the sea, running miles inland, emptying it, running back, filling it again, running and emptying it again. Why don't you stop, and let *me* bring in the tide?"

In that moment I saw that all my life I had been striving to meet standards of perfection through my own efforts, seeking by hard work to bring in the Kingdom of God. Now, as I saw the bankruptcy of this position, I said, "God, I have made a mess of my life. I turn it over to you and I will do anything you want me to do."

Afterward, my first thought was that I should reveal myself to my wife. It took six weeks to muster the courage to do this, for I feared she would be disappointed in "the real me" and would never forgive me. But when I at last told her of my years of deep loneliness, of my fears, lust, cowardice, and resentment, her reaction was to ask, "How can *I* change so that it will be easier for you to talk freely with me?"

We entered into a new relationship. To my bewildered amazement, she could love the "me" behind my facade. And with this new love from my wife came a corresponding love from God. Telling another human being about myself had melted my pride, and I felt known and loved, forgiven and restored to fellowship both with God and with my wife.

I was learning to accept myself as God had accepted me, and consequently I was willing to be known by my fellowmen. More and more I was free to allow people to see me as a garden variety of sinner.

Soon after the encounter with my wife, I was at a ministers' meeting. Someone commented, "Lee, you look happy." "I am," I said. He asked why, and I replied, "Do you really want to know?"

He hesitated a moment, then said, "Yes." I told him what had happened, and finally he said, "You are telling my story." In a moment we were praying together. Three weeks later I met him again, and his radiant smile testified to a similar miracle in his life.

I began to make restitution—sending checks to people from whom I had stolen, apologizing to my college dean for cheating, asking forgiveness from friends for lies and unkindness. To some of my church officers I apologized for bigotry and autocratic ways, for appointing committees "loaded" in favor of my plans and ideas.

A new joy developed among us and people began to be different. Stubbornness gave way to the kind of love Paul describes in I Corinthians 13. Prayer groups, quest groups, and retreats came into being.

Everything was not smooth sailing, of course. In my enthusiasm I made many mistakes, giving people the impression that *I* had achieved an experience which *they* needed. Some fellow ministers whispered that my exuberance would "soon pass," or that it was too bad that Lee had "gone religious." But others listened hungrily to what had happened, and some joined me in the exciting quest.

Previously I had felt that the coming of God's Kingdom was

dependent on my hard work. But now I saw that this was God's world and He was running it. As someone has put it, "I resigned from being general manager of the universe." My only responsibility was to do God's will for me moment by moment.

My life took on a leisurely fullness. I did less, but less was more! My preaching and pastoral work had been marked by pressure to interest people in social action, to get people converted and quickened in the way of Christ. But now my emphasis changed: I began to proclaim God's love, and to show God at work in the world. It was not my job to change people, but to bear witness—from the Bible, from history, from current events, and from my own heart—to the work and grace of God.

Lee Whiston had stepped off the pedestal. My people knew me now as a sinner who was willing to be honest about himself, to be forgiven constantly, and to live in deep fellowship with his parishioners.

It is thirty-three years since I began this new way of life, and I am still learning. I am on the trail, but still have far to go. The excitement is in the journey, not the arrival.

A few months ago someone surprised me with the question, "Are you a different kind of person than you used to be?" My reply was, "No, I'm still a fellow who wants to be praised, who wants to resent and to withdraw from encounter." But in this I am different: day by day I tell my wife and my Christian friends what kind of person I am. I call on God and on people for help. Day by day God gives victory and forgiveness. The amazing miracle is how much and how often He uses me—and this is always in accordance with my willingness to put my faith in Him and Him alone, and to be obedient, implicitly and immediately. I am only a channel. God is the power, and to Him belongs the praise.   —*October, 1966*

It's good news when a person moves from a dead end onto

life's high road, when power replaces powerlessness and when love supplants pressure. When this happens to a clergyman and he admits it, it's not only news but headlines. Lee Whiston shatters our false image of the clergy. His life is marked by openness and the disarming quality that breaks down barriers and builds new edifices of faith. Lee and his wife Irma have in recent years plunged into an extraordinary ministry—leading conferences and retreats for people of all ages. They have a particular feeling for fellow pastors, and have been very helpful to them. In addition to all this, Lee has been turning out a delightful series of Bible study guides for teen-agers.

Chapter 26

■

THE HEALING OF THE HEART

by Jeanne Carruthers

It stole upon my husband in his forty-ninth year, that creeping death of mind and body, *cerebralarteriosclerosis,* robbing him of his ability to communicate with others, bringing a glazed, unfocused look into his eyes—eyes that had laughed with me, had looked at me with love for twenty-five years.

His skilled physician's fingers began to fumble and grope aimlessly. His medical career was over; our beloved home in India was gone forever.

I could scarcely bear to hear his slow, shuffling walk—to see the dragging left foot of this man who used to stride from bed to bed, bringing healing to the sick among the wards of the mission hospital. And then his faltering speech and inability to remember words brought on intolerable frustration and unutterable loneliness.

Our earthly love was dead. Everything that had nourished it was gone; the strength on which I had always leaned, the brilliant mind, the gentle physician's compassion—so spendthrift of time and energy—the over-brimming enthusiasm of planning for the future.

In agony I prayed, *O God, it is more than I can bear. In desperation I dare to ask of Thee, give me in place of these ashes Thine own love for him.*

Bruce lay asleep in his hospital bed, almost completely helpless because of a stroke, and I knelt beside him, holding his hand, listening to his breathing. Suddenly, as I prayed, I realized that I was not just "standing by," nor just watching him suffer, but in the mysterious workings of the love of God, I was dying with him. With the death of my earthly, physical love, there came also the death of every self-centered desire and passion. Fear died, too—the fear of illness and death. All that was left in him was the breath of God, and all that remained in me was the breathing of God's love.

I left the hospital there in Canada and returned to my job in New York, seemingly alone. But everything had changed. I knew that I had "died"—and come back in the love of God.

The city looked the same, its streets being ripped up by a giant drill, rocks and dirt spewing from cavernous jaws of a monstrous crane, pounding trucks and swishing motor cars, people elbowing and stepping on each other and not stopping to notice.

But what I saw was the saffron and gold sunlight, dawning silently on the city in a blaze of joy. I saw peace like the rivers that flow around Manhattan Island, bearing on an irresistible current all the cargoes and burdens of men. I saw the Kingdom of God, "which is peace, righteousness, and joy."

All at once I wanted to seize the hand of one of those hurrying people and say, *Look, let me tell you about the Kingdom of God. It's the only thing that matters. My husband lost everything because of illness—all the things that seem so important: car and home, prestige, titles of respect, honorary degrees. He is lying now in the valley of the shadow of death. His mind and his body are shattered.*

And then I wanted to go on, *You may not believe this, but none of those things really counts. God is breathing through my husband. Love is holding him by the hand, and he has everything that matters.*

If I could only have expressed to someone what I now saw in Bruce, after he had stared death in the face for five long years! If I could only have communicated that now he lived serenely in the assurance that his name was written in heaven, that his patient smile spoke with the tongues of angels, and that his spirit moved in an atmosphere where there is no fear and no death!

In the midst of a mortal illness his whole being cried out, *Don't you understand? This means that love has won. Nothing can separate me from the love of God in Christ Jesus. I know that there is nothing to fear in all the earth.*

Every month I went to Canada to be with Bruce in the hospital. In October he greeted me with all the old warmth. In November he had another stroke, which paralyzed his left side. Then pneumonia set in.

As our children and I stood by through those last, agonizing hours, I thought back on our years of happiness together. At the time of our marriage Bruce and I had given our lives to Christ, and a year later we had made the decision that took us into more than twenty years of companionship and work among the people of India. As I bent low to share with him the last earthly experience, I once more dedicated myself to that same mission of the Church which Bruce had served with all his mind and heart and strength.

And then the moment arrived when the last strong breath left his body, and I knew that Bruce was living the eternal life promised to the redeemed in Christ.

An eternity to explore the truths and mysteries of God! I thought of his keen scientific mind, which was always probing for truth in the field of medicine; of his delight in new ideas; his love of beauty. I saw him purified of all pride and ambition, with no ugly scars, no memory of five years of illness and disability—nothing but absolute freedom. With these thoughts, a wave of inexpressible joy swept over me.

He seemed to stand beside me, radiantly alive, repeating again the words of Elizabeth Barrett Browning that had brought us so much pleasure: "I love thee with the breath, smiles, tears of all my life—and, if God choose, I shall but love thee better after death."

To all whose loved ones are suffering from incurable disease; to all who cannot accept NO for an answer to their prayers for healing, my husband and I can now say from experience, God be praised! Sickness can be so transformed by the love of Christ that it is not unto death, but for the glory of God.

The Lord Jesus Christ, who had gone before us through the whole experience of death, deliberately, in the full strength of His manhood, once more had triumphed. It was the most complete of healings—the healing of the heart!   —*July, 1959*

The late Dr. L. Bruce Carruthers served as a medical missionary in India for twenty-one years, during which time he trained more than four hundred doctors for service in rural areas of that country. His widow wrote this story of the last months of his life in the hope that it would help readers concerned with healing to "go beyond the personal into a spiritual experience." It is one of the most beautiful stories ever to appear in FAITH AT WORK.

Chapter 27

■

NOTHING LIKE LOVE

By Adeline Trapp
Teacher, New York City*

Many of us, in dealing with difficult and disturbed children, presuppose that these children were either "born bad" or for some unknown reason became bad. We mete out punishment for unacceptable behavior, either by beating them, or telling them to "shut up," or by detailing their faults. Then we are perplexed that the badness isn't spanked out, or that after hearing their faults, children don't mend their ways with this new knowledge so generously given. We punish, threaten, cajole, ignore, and try a million and one tricks to manipulate children into the kind of behavior patterns we want them to adopt.

Sometimes children are threatened to such a degree and become so terrified of the consequences of bad behavior that they literally cease to function. Everything in life becomes a potential source of punishment, and they are rendered emotionally, socially, and spiritually more dead than alive. Others become so hostile that they do unto all others they meet very much as they have been done to.

Often their behavior is so perplexing and beyond our under-

*Since this story was written, the author has taken a job in Europe.

standing that we are rendered immobile. The moment they sense
our confusion and inability to act, they behave even worse. Those
of us who don't know how to handle difficult and defiant behavior and who choose to ignore it soon find that we have lost
the respect of the entire group.

When we return evil for evil we perpetuate a vicious cycle. We
may seem to be successful for a time, but the moment this kind
of authority turns his back, the antisocial behavior begins again.
There is no permanent change. Is there no answer? Jesus Christ
said that He is the Way, the Truth, and the Life and with Him
we find that *one way* that is the solution for all that appears impossible.

I have taught for ten years in a New York City public school,
and have met a continual stream of disturbed children ranging
from those who are shy, quiet, and withdrawn, filled with fear
and hatred, to aggressive, destructive, defiant youngsters who fight
everyone and everything in sight.

I immediately recognized how impossible teaching would be
under these conditions, realized my own inadequacy in the face
of emotional illness, and knew that I would either have to find
outside help for these children or struggle in a most ineffective
manner and accomplish nothing. The psychological and sociolog-
ical services available within the school and in outside agencies
were so overloaded that it was useless to fill out referral forms.
And even then, the sickness was so deep-seated and powerful that
it seemed to me that difficulties of such enormity were beyond
the limited capabilities of people. These were no run-of-the-mill
problems. Only God could handle this sort of thing.

I prayed without ceasing. I prayed for understanding, wisdom,
patience, the strength necessary to be able to withstand the constant barrage of hate, and for the right words and actions for each
day's encounters.

I remember watching a little first-grader in the lunchroom.

She threw food at the other children, cursed her teacher, and frequently ran riot with the adults in hot pursuit. We once met head on and she shot me a withering, "You say one more word and I'll take my shoe off and let you have it so hard, you won't know what hit you!"

The following September I had a second grade class and you can guess who I inherited. She apparently remembered me, too, for she took one look at her teacher and began to cry. Though she was somewhat subdued, she still employed her unfriendly tactics. One day after a particularly trying episode, I sent for her mother. What a revelation! She stormed into the room and slapped her little girl around, using a continual stream of abusive language. I got her out as quickly as I could and found my attitude toward the child completely changed. I apologized for calling her mother in, said I had no idea what she was up against, and promised that no matter what happened, I would never report her errors to her mother again. I'll never forget the look of utter disbelief she gave me. It might seem that what I said would give rise to even worse behavior. Perhaps fear of her mother had kept her behaving as well as she did, though so far below standard. But the fear was apparently the cause. She immediately changed and three weeks later her mother came to tell me how delightful she had become at home. She became one of the sweetest, brightest little girls I've ever worked with.

For almost two years a little third-grader had been unable to remember one reading word. He hated his fellow classmates, and was a very frightened, unhappy, and lonely little boy. He was a trial over which I often prayed, yet nothing I did seemed to work. Second grade had been impossible and third wasn't much better. Then, in April of the second year, he told me that he bullied and frightened the children so that they would not get him first. The following week he recalled an incident when he was three. While he was waiting somewhere for his mother, a woman annoyed him and he called her "fat pig." In retaliation, she donned some sort of mask and frightened the wits out of him, so that when a boy in the class made himself a small mask, this little boy picked up a chair to hit him. This had apparently been the trouble because the anger disappeared and in the few remaining months he covered more than two years of reading, retaining every word and comprehending well.

I am unable to explain just how and why, but I have seen children change right before my eyes, and I have watched myself change, too. Some of the changes came quickly and others took a long, long time. There were days when it all seemed so impossible that I was ready to concede that there were forces in operation here that were even out of God's jurisdiction. But He proved me wrong.

When anger and resentment swelled within me, rather than count to ten I recalled every verse of Scripture that I had committed to memory, and gradually I found that I was beginning to return good for evil. I learned a lesson that was a bitter pill to swallow. I was my biggest problem. Many of the glaring faults in my personality were revealed to me, and when I was able to ask God to remove my blocks of fear and anger, I saw corresponding changes in the children.

I hated many of the attitudes and traits which I saw in these children because I hated these attitudes and traits in myself. Only God made it possible for me to come to understand, love, and accept them regardless of their behavior. I did not scream back at them. I set the necessary limits which they actually craved. I listened respectfully to all they had to say. We had parties, took trips, and I gave classwork so simple that everyone could finally taste the sweet fruits of success.

In a nutshell, I treated them as I wanted them to treat me and everyone else. I was not only teacher, judge and jury, mediator, and distributor of band-aids, but the authority whom they could "test out" to find the answers they sought about people; then to trust, and finally to emulate. I can only conclude that we adults make children whatever they come to be.

It is no wonder that children are as confused, hostile, and vindictive as they are. When they reveal some of the lethal blows that have been dealt them, physically and emotionally, one begins to understand the process of cause and effect. And yet if they continue to seek revenge, justifiable as it may seem, the vicious cycle repeats itself, and they treat all others, and eventually their own children, in the same sick way.

We seek answers to this dilemma. The colleges struggle with their profound theories, medical men develop drugs and elaborate machinery in their attempt to detect and eliminate physical causes, and psychiatrists probe the mind attempting to understand the difficulties and effect cures.

There is only one way to stop this process and that is to meet it head on with love, to absorb the anger and hatred, and not to become sick with it ourselves.

Only the knowledge that Christ has this kind of love for me and everyone else made it possible for me to have it, too. I have found that as I forgive a child his trespasses, he forgives mine (and they are many), and we learn and grow together. As I give my attention to children, they listen to me, and we come to know one another. As I seek ways to help them over rough spots, they reach out to each other to make the going a little easier for all concerned.

For two years I worked with a special class of fifteen very disturbed second-graders, and I watched this way of love change even them. I knew that somehow I had come upon something so powerful and so redemptive that it defies description. Nothing can stand in the face of God's love and nothing can stop it. It cuts through every defense mechanism, every fear and resentment. It heals the deepest wounds and creates new personalities.

And these new personalities are good ones. The fruits of love are smiling faces, concern for other people, and the inner strength to take life as it comes and deal effectively with it.

It requires the realization that one cannot stand alone. When I was able to admit that I did not have the answers and when I took this to God asking His help, He was there immediately. Time and time again He caused me to look deep within myself—a painful process but one that tears up the problems and brings them into the light of day. The more I understood myself, the more I grew to understand children. I wish I could say that my anger and resentment have completely disappeared, but it would not be true. They always cause me great trouble until I give them over to Jesus. This is a continual process for me. I give them to Him, and He does the work.

This way of love is given to all who request it. It cannot be bought, or earned with great deeds. It cannot be learned in a college course. It comes quickest to one who stands the lowest. It is a way of living that I am eternally grateful to have found.

—January, 1965

Sometimes in dealing with children—especially difficult ones— we find ourselves out of our depth and are driven to applying spiritual principles. It may come as a shock that they actually work! Addie Trapp has proved the efficacy of such an approach, not only as a one-shot deal but over the long haul. Those who are familiar with public schools in the congested inner-city will realize just how difficult a problem Addie faced, and how meaningful are her discoveries.

Chapter 28

■

MOTOR FAILS—GOD SUCCEEDS

by Merrell Vories Hitotsuyanagi
Founder of the Omi Brotherhood, Omi-Hachiman, Japan

During the early months of the occupation of Japan, after World War II, I was asked to give a series of lectures on Christianity and Democracy in a neighboring province. Because of poor railway service at the time, an automobile was sent to bring me to the town—a four-hour drive. Setting out early in the morning in order to arrive by noon, we had proceeded for only about twenty-five minutes when the car stopped abruptly on a rural road, far from help or even a telephone.

The chauffeur tried in vain to start the engine again and then began frantically searching for the cause of the trouble. A number of cars and trucks passed, but no one paused to offer help. Finally a jeep carrying three GIs came up behind us, stopped, and asked the driver—in English—if this road were the one they ought to be on. Since he could not understand them, I jumped out and offered to help.

The young Americans nearly burst their skins at sight of what they presumed was an American in the wilderness. They scarcely listened to my assurance that they were on the right road. The lieutenant, who sat beside the driver of the jeep, shouted: "What are *you* doing in this *blankety-blank* country, and where are you headed?" When I explained my plight he volunteered to give me a lift to the nearest railway station, so I could proceed by train. I jumped in with the third GI on the back seat and, as soon as the jeep started, the young officer turned to me again, inquiring, "Did you say you've been in Japan more than forty years? How in —— have you stood it among these *blankety-blank,* bloodthirsty barbarians?"

I smiled. "How long have *you* been in Japan?" I asked.

"We've been here six weeks," he said.

"In that case," I went on, "perhaps I'm a little better acquainted with the people than you."

Then, as they conveyed me to Maibara, I proceeded to give them some facts about Japan and its people. As we neared the station some forty minutes later, the young man beside me brought his hand down on my knee with a friendly whack, exclaiming, with a laugh, "Then the Japs are human, like the rest of us?" And the lieutenant added warmly, "Say, Sir, I'm sure glad your car broke down today. We've been getting it all wrong, and it might have made our service a failure!"

The Station Master himself now hastily conducted me to the platform. "Ordinarily," he assured me, "the next train would be an hour and a half from now, but there's a *special,* ready to start in three minutes!"

The "special" proved to be a trainload of Japanese ex-soldiers returning home from defeat. It was so crowded that the Station Master had to command a window to be opened through which he shoved me into the train, and had he not been an old friend of mine, I would never have got on at all.

The car was packed with young men, ranging from seventeen to twenty-five years of age. As the train began to roll, up jumped a man of about forty, evidently the ex-officer in charge, who began a harangue. He reminded the boys that they had been seeing the ruins of their homeland along the way and declared that all the suffering they had endured had been brought on because of the Emperor's ambitions. Their only hope, he asserted, lay in Communism—which meant that they, the young and strong remnant, must rise up, overthrow the government, and rebuild the nation on this new system.

The speaker looked at me more than once but supposed that I could not understand him—else why should the Station Master have had to put me aboard personally? When I had stood it as long as I could, I asked, "Excuse me, sir, but when were you born?" Such was his surprise at hearing me speak Japanese that he couldn't think up an answer and blurted out, "1904"—which happened to be just one year before my arrival in Japan.

While he paused in astonishment, I pointed out that *that* made him only one year older in experience in Japan than I; and that, furthermore, while he might not have made much of a study of the social and economic problems of his country, I had come to Japan at twenty-four, and had become intimately acquainted with all aspects of its life. "Besides," I added, "during the late war you have been absent on distant fronts, while I have been here all through and have received inside information from statesmen, in addition to my own observations. Therefore I suggest that I be allowed to take over for a while."

Dumbfounded, the Communist relapsed into silence, while the surprised young men gave their rapt attention to my version of the cause of the war, the actions of the responsible military clique, and to what I felt to be the only hopeful and rational means of reconstruction.

Just as my hour-long "lecture" ended, we came to the place where I was to alight. My young hearers all arose and bowed, and made profuse expressions of thanks for learning the real conditions of their beloved land and their true hope of recovery.

Without missing my original appointment, I had thus far been granted the privilege of rendering service to two groups equally important— and all because of the *apparent* disaster of a stalled auto. The "disaster" also provided a particularly telling illustration to enrich the lectures of the following three days.

There was a *fourth* "by-product" on my return journey. The official who had planned the project explained apologetically that he felt the auto he had sent for me was too unreliable, even though repaired, for the trip back, and so I was sent home by train.

The first train now proved to be so jam-packed that I could not even get a toe-hold. I had to wait two hours for the next one only to discover that this was equally crowded—except for a reserved coach "for the use of occupational personnel."

As it was getting late, I ventured to ask if I might be permitted to enter this special car. There was an argument between the official responsible for the car and the conductor of the train, who opposed my suggestion, but finally I was aboard. Then, when the inner door was opened, I discovered that the coach was occupied entirely by American Negroes—although there were several vacant seats. The man in charge of the company shook his head emphatically in the negative at the possibility of a white man's entering. So it appeared that I must get off, after all. Only the train had now begun to move, and the Japanese conductor said I would *have* to stay on till we reached the next stop.

As he and I stood in the entry conversing in Japanese, the officer who had blocked my entrance presently motioned to me to come in and indicated a vacant seat across the aisle from his own.

He then started asking me questions. How long had I been in Japan? Had he heard me use the word *"Christian"* in the Japanese conversation? I told him a little about the work of the Omi Brotherhood and he became quite interested and friendly.

Then a younger man, two rows ahead, turned around. "May I ask you a question, Sir?"

So I went up and sat beside him. "Did I hear you say *'Christian'* just now?" he also wanted to know. And, getting my assurance, he went on, "When I started on this trip this morning, I had a deep wish that today I might meet somebody who could answer a question that has been bothering me for months. You look old enough to have had lots of experience. Maybe you are the one I was hoping to meet. My trouble is that I can't figure out how, if there is a God in this world, He could let such an awful thing as this war happen. I've been worrying about this question until I've just about lost my faith."

Here of course was the reason I had had to return by train! Again, the weak auto was needed! The twenty-three-year-old Negro—a man of fine physique and intelligent appearance—listened intently as I admitted that I also had suffered from such a quandary and surmised a great many others had. I told him that, although I was not a theologian and my solution might not be the best one, my conviction was as follows:

The Creator made all men whoever they be with freedom of will, responsible for their own choices. If we were controlled by Him in all our actions, as a puppet is manipulated with strings, we would not be *men,* and there would be no true morality in human society. God does not "permit" wars, in the sense of condoning them. He has spoken against hatred and murder, by the words of prophets, and has given us a perfect model for human life in the life and teachings of Jesus Christ. But we ourselves have failed to heed His counsel or follow His way. Selfishness, pride, greed, fear, and all our weaknesses have led us far from His plans for us, and these have caused competition and warfare between man and man and nation and nation. *We* are the ones who make war upon our brother-men—who also are the children of God, potentially. "God's law is *love,*" I concluded; "but *we disobey it.*"

The young man said he had never thought of this explanation, that he now saw it clearly, and was *so glad I had been "sent" to that particular train.* Then he called to one of his friends and strongly advised him, if he had any problems or worries, to lay them before "this man who has just cleared up my own great anxiety."

Pretty soon a group gathered round us, and the remainder of my journey home became a fellowship of sharing and testimony. At Omi-Hachiman station some of the men jumped out onto the platform and held the train overtime while they snapped my photo, and the young fellow who had started the episode insisted that I accept his fountain pen "as a memento of this most happy day of my life."   —*December, 1954*

The late Merrell Vories was an American who spent most of his life in Japan. So closely did he identify with his adopted people that he became a Japanese citizen and assumed his wife's surname. The fruits of this close identification and selfless service are very much in evidence in Japan today. The Omi Brotherhood is a community which provides education and work for many Japanese, and a laboratory in which countless numbers have made the leap of faith and committed themselves to Jesus Christ. In a day when the traditional "missionary" image has become sadly tarnished, Merrell Vories shines like gold.

Chapter 29

■

I SHARE THEIR SUFFERING

by Charlotte Tan
Medical Doctor, New York City

After three months at the medical center, I had had enough. I was so depressed that I cried out one day, "I just can't stand it any longer." No matter how hard we tried, we couldn't save those little children.

I'm a pediatrician, you see, and for eleven years have worked at a large medical center where most of the patients are victims of cancer. Unfortunately, children get cancer too, and in most cases there simply is no cure. When they first come to the hospital, they are all as cute as can be, but then, one by one, most of them die, no matter how hard we doctors work to save them.

Then I faced a simple question. "Someone has to help those children," I said to myself. "If you don't, who will?" Suddenly I realized that this was to be my mission field.

I had wanted to be a medical missionary ever since I turned my life over to Christ during my second year in medical school in China. With my new life came a new purpose and new values, and I determined not only to apply medical science to the sick but also to help them come to know my Lord.

I came to the United States for post-graduate training, but

when I was ready to return to China, the doors were closed and I found myself at the cancer clinic instead. I felt it my duty to witness to my faith in Christ, but I'm ashamed to say I was quite ineffective. My eyes were blind to the needs of others and my heart insensitive to the leading of the Holy Spirit.

My witness was just words. Before I would speak of Christ to the parents of one of my patients, I would always look at his chart to see what religion was indicated, whether Protestant, Catholic, or Jewish. I restricted my "witnessing" to Protestants, thinking that they would better understand what I had to say. Now I deliberately do not look at the chart. I want to talk to people simply as human beings and to share their sufferings with them.

It took me a long time to realize that there is no easy answer to suffering, and people don't welcome one who comes with oversimplified answers. Suffering is the deepest mystery of life. What the sufferer needs is not someone who tells him, "Cheer up; things could be worse," but someone who will stand beside him and say, in the words of Oswald Chambers, "I don't see how you are going through this; it is black and desperate, but I will wait with you." Most of all, it is my privilege to help people see that our Lord doesn't leave us to suffer alone, nor will He fail to help us in our need.

God has a plan for every one of His children. There is really no need for the God of all creation to justify Himself before men, nor is it proper for us to demand that He explain Himself to us. As Isaiah said, "For my thoughts are not your thoughts, neither are your ways my ways, says the Lord. For as the heavens are higher than the earth, so are my ways higher than your ways and my thought than your thoughts."

A good Jewish friend reminded me once, "God is too wise to make a mistake." Yes, God is a loving God, despite the mystery of suffering. Even His own Son, Jesus, received no answer when

He cried out on the Cross, "My God, my God, *why?*" He received no answer, but for us He is the answer. It is in Christ that we know God loves the world. And it is my responsibility to help those who are suffering to see it as a challenge—that men's extremities are God's opportunities.

Now that I am a mother myself, I know the agony and terror parents must go through when their children suffer from some dreadful disease. Very few parents I have met have enough faith to meet the crisis when they discover that their child's disease is malignant. Often they are bitter and resentful. Occasionally a brave mother may ask, through her tears, "Why?"

Instead of answering her with "words," as I used to do, I now know that words won't do, and instead I slip my arm around her and say, "I don't know, but let's pray." Prayer is the best way to identify with them, and God Almighty can comfort them as I cannot.

One day I prayed with the mother of a very sick child. When we lifted our heads, her face was wet with tears, but she was smiling. "How did you know," she asked, "that this was just what I needed?" Later she told me that her husband wanted to ask me some questions. I went up to the children's ward and found him there, but he didn't really have any questions. It was simply that his wife wanted him to pray with me too. She told me the next morning that for the first time in her life God was real to her.

We prayed together several times after that. Her little daughter was in terrible pain, and I prayed for her as if she were my own child, that God would give her enough strength to bear it.

I always make my prayers specific: not, "Lord, heal little Carol," but, "Help her get over her stomach-ache tonight." I consider myself part of the suffering family and try to say what I think the child would pray at this moment.

There is a beautiful little chapel in our hospital. I like to take parents to this quiet place to talk, and when we're through it is only natural to ask the parents if they will pray with me.

A Jewish couple brought their eight-year-old boy all the way from Florida for consultation. I treated him for awhile, then the time came for them to return home. It was in the chapel, when I finished making the arrangements for their return, that we prayed together. I said, "Dear Lord Jesus, our cultural backgrounds and religious beliefs may be different, but You are the One who loves us all."

There were others in the chapel at the time, so I included them in my prayer too. I didn't know if they were Jewish, Protestant, or Catholic. I only knew that God was with us all. And when I finished I saw tears in everyone's eyes. One man said, "Praise the Lord!" The Jewish father kissed my hand and whispered, "We will always pray for you."

A five-year-old Jewish boy, quite precocious, suddenly found himself blind because of a malignancy behind his eyes. When I asked him quietly, "Have you ever prayed?" he answered, "No, how do I pray? I wish someone had told me about prayers before this."

I had treated twelve-year-old Janet for several months, and found that her mother was a faithful Christian. It became a game between us that each time she came to the clinic she would have a Bible verse ready to recite and I had to have one too. It was a wonderful chance to brush up on Bible memory work, and Janet had transformed her illness from a problem to a challenge to her whole family.

One boy, thirteen, was with us for awhile and no one in his family or the hospital staff could control him. I was afraid to talk to him because of his wildness, but finally my guilty conscience would allow me to ignore him no longer. I went into his room and he was moaning in deep pain. "Jack," I asked, "have you ever heard John 3:16?" "Yes, but I don't remember it, so please tell me." So I did, and when I had explained its truth to him, I asked him if he wanted to ask the Lord Jesus to come into his heart. He did, and we prayed together. The very next day, he went to be with the Lord.

Johnny's parents brought in their four-year-old son for examination one day. He was pale and very sick and as I was about to perform a bone-marrow test to determine whether he had leukemia, Johnny's dad said, with deep emotion, "I hope you'll pray with us that Johnny doesn't have what we're afraid of."

I didn't know how seriously he believed in prayer but I answered, "Yes, I will pray for you because I believe God answers prayer."

When the test proved to be positive, Mr. Post asked me dozens of questions about the disease. I answered each question honestly, but at last I said, "Human knowledge is so limited. Don't put your hope in what we can do. Trust in God." He squeezed my hand. "I believe that," he said. "That's our only hope."

I knew that he and Mrs. Post were Christians so when they went on vacation that summer, I sent them my printed testimony that had been published by the American Tract Society. They wrote back, "The first time we met you, we noticed something different about you and now we know why. It is God in you."

As Johnny's illness progressed, he needed many blood transfusions. At first he cried bitterly and pleaded, "Don't hurt me." I told him, "Johnny, I'll let you in on a secret. Every time I give a child a needle, I pray to God that I will only make him better and not hurt him." When it was over, he smiled, "It didn't hurt a bit." You could see the peace of God shining in his eyes. Then he added, "I wish all children had faith in God like me, because I'm not afraid."

Many months later, when Johnny passed away, his father said, "The Lord answered our prayers. He not only healed Johnny; He healed my wife and me as well." They came out

stronger in faith than before, and are seeking every opportunity to serve God.
                                                                    —*March, 1964*

Dr. Charlotte Tan looks more like a movie star than a physician, yet her article unconsciously reveals an inner beauty even more striking than the physical. Clearly, she has a unique opportunity to serve through her profession, yet her story provides a pattern for anyone who is willing to show forth God's love and comfort in a pain-wracked world.

Chapter 30

∎

THE MARKET PLACE:
TESTING GROUND FOR FAITH

by Robert S. Ellis
Businessman, Villanova, Pennsylvania

When I entered the business world, I wasn't concerned about
the Christian faith or any other faith. In fact, I was an atheist.
Some years later, after I had given my life to Christ, I asked Him
if He wanted me in the ministry or some "full-time Christian
service," but the answer was, *Stay in the market place.*

If Christianity is practical and relevant, it must be just as
applicable in the market place as it is in a monastery. If it isn't,
we should all become monks. But then who would support the
monasteries? I personally owe the clergy a great deal, and know
that many of them live dedicated and sacrificial lives, but a
football team is not made up solely of coaches. Much as it needs
them, it also needs players in the field.

Jesus chose His disciples from among laymen, and gave us
many parables which dignify labor. It is clear that our Lord
intended His teaching to be as relevant to business, the family,
and the community, as it is to the organized Church. The market
place is, in fact, the testing ground for the faith of most men
and many women.

Business gives us the opportunity to contribute to the physical growth of society, God's human and material creation. Man cannot live by bread alone, but neither can he live without it. Business enables us to support our families, institutions, schools, churches, hospitals, the causes we believe in—*His* causes.

On the negative side, competition is a mixed blessing. It makes for progress: better products, better services, inventiveness, lower costs, more goods available to more people, a growing economy. But over-intense competition can lead to a lowering of the moral standard and the loss of human dignity through a thousand ways of cutting corners. At this point, the would-be follower of Christ faces a real challenge. Shall he compromise as he sees others doing, and if not, can he survive? This is precisely the point where the Christian faith *is* relevant to business.

When I became a Christian, I had to revise my whole set of standards. This was limiting, at first. Not being able to mislead or bully others seemed an unnecessary handicap, and it *would* have been but for one thing: Jesus makes available resources and insights which are ours to appropriate—His guidance and power. I don't mean that He will give us an unfair advantage over our competition, but if we are asking Him what He wants us to do, and sincerely acting upon what guidance He gives, He will work out His plan in our lives.

God's plan for me got off to an unpromising start. Father died when I was eight so Mother and I had many problems getting through the depression. I emerged from childhood with a strong determination to get ahead, and a king-size chip on my shoulder. Although I always managed to have a few intimate friends, my "strong personality" rubbed most people the wrong way.

The drive I had somehow acquired got me an engineering degree at night school, although this long, difficult period was interrupted by a recession and World War II, in which I was a B-17 navigator in the European theatre. Just before combat, the girl I love consented to marry me, and this was a powerful, sweetening influence in my life. Bunny is a realist and a sound confidante, but she also has the capacity for strong love, support, and encouragement.

During my late teens and early twenties, I passed from childhood faith to skepticism to atheism. Just before the war, I came under the persuasive influence of Dr. Norman Vincent Peale, for which I am now very grateful. At first tentatively and then confidently, I began to accept the existence of God and the possibility of His being a benign influence. This was a good beginning, and helped me to maintain a sense of proportion during combat in which we lost half our flying personnel. It often seemed that nothing but the law of averages was operating in that situation, and I saw men of all faiths displaying courage, being shot down, or getting through unhurt, seemingly without regard to what they believed about God. Tragedy was no respecter of persons and I was unable to pray for safety—only for the ability to be competent under fire.

Just after the victory over our wartime enemies, we seemed to be under immediate threat from our former allies, and the prospect of another war, this one to be nuclear, spelled out for me clearly that there is no permanent security in men or their treaties and agreements. Back in New York I was beginning to be a little more successful, and with Bunny also making a good income as a legal secretary, we could begin to afford a few things. Nevertheless, I could already see that the mere desire for and possession of things did not guarantee permanent happiness, security, or significance, any more than did humanism. My extreme competitiveness didn't always win friends and influence people, either. Clearly, I needed a new dimension in my life, and I'm glad it never took the form of desire for escape.

At last I graduated from college. Formal education and working for a living had been taking virtually all my time. I now set out in earnest to find out if faith in God was relevant. God probably existed, I thought, but did this make any real difference in our lives? I believed Jesus had been dead for some two thousand years, and that He'd been little more than a kind and good teacher.

Through a seemingly chance circumstance, our love of good music, we visited Calvary Episcopal Church one Sunday in 1948, and that ended our shopping. We had never before heard of Dr. Sam Shoemaker, but we never went to another church until 1952 when he was called to Pittsburgh and we to Mexico City. Those four years completely changed my life. No longer did I consider all Christians "fuzzy thinkers." There were many logical, intelligent minds in that church, and in its many fellowship groups were people who were far smarter than I, yet there I found clear-eyed, unashamed faith. It wasn't rammed down my throat, but it gave forth the light of surety, confidence, experience, joy, and as it turned out it was rooted in dialogue with the Jesus who I'd been so sure was dead.

One manifestation of the faith in this crowd was undeserved love for me, and patience (bordering on amusement) with my silly and futile attempts to beat down with argument that which they knew from experience to be true. What they had was attractive! I had to experiment, even if it was foolish, to see if I could find this radiant faith.

Meanwhile, Sam's reasonable, logical preaching and private talks (he found time for people) were sinking stiffening piles deep down into the quicksand of my unbelief. He knew that honest doubts must be dealt with fairly, even while watching for the real reason behind the proffered reasons we give for fighting off real contact with God.

In the end I turned my life over to Christ in the greatest decision I ever made. Though I claim no unblemished record of faithfulness to Him, His record of faithfulness to me is unspotted. Though it sometimes contains some hard lessons, and always demands further growth and understanding from me, I wouldn't trade this relationship for anything. It is the source of all I hold dear and important.

As an engineer whose work is selling heavy machinery, I have agonized over the preparation of sales presentations when I felt inadequate personally, or when the obstacles seemed unsurmountable. Too much of this kind of pressure can lead to the excessive use of alcohol, happy pills, perpetual TV viewing, and various other escapes. The keystone of my faith, as it applies to the question of adequacy, is that *Jesus Christ will make me adequate to do whatever He wants me to do.*

Obviously, this may leave out some courses of action I might have selected, but since He is in control of my life, I'm counting on Him to open the right doors. This makes anxiety and pills unnecessary. He will not hold me responsible for tasks He has not given me the equipment to handle, but He will enable me to do anything that fits in with His purposes. Added to present power for the day, He gives us forgiveness of the past, the security of His love, and everlasting life for the future. To take this to heart means there is nothing to fear! We can be buoyant, free, alive! Now are we truly free to be creative and imaginative about our work.

Of course, it is one thing to hear these things from another, but quite different to experience them ourselves. The first time we put our weight down on Him and find that He is really there, it seems a wondrous miracle. We may say, "My Lord, it really is true. You are here!" After that, things begin to happen.

I was encouraged to begin praying for anyone I hated. I began with the hardest one—my boss! Resentment is the most corrosive element we can allow into our personalities. It makes us fearful and guilty. It can ruin us. It was amazing as I prayed for my boss to watch him become a friend and actually begin to help me! This transforming of hatred into friendship has happened many times since.

I suppose resentment thrives in business because we are competing for money, prestige, and power—the things in which we seek to find security, significance, and satisfaction. But when we find these three *s's* in God, we are free to pray for people because they no longer have the power to threaten us. We can afford to forgive and to love them because He first forgave and loved us. People seeing the change in us then ask why we are different, and we then get a chance to relate them to Him.

Not everyone comes around when we stop being resentful. Jesus didn't hate, but He was still hated by some because of what He stood for. Many of Christ's teachings have to do with the way we do business—not if we should, but how? If our methods are not perceptibly different from those of non-believers, there is no witness. The pressures to succeed are very intense. How do we stand fast? We are dependent on His strength rather than ours, as in the question of adequacy. We pray, "Lead us not into temptation, but deliver us from evil."

Things can get pretty sticky. I once was threatened with jail for not going along with dishonesty. I was scared to death! But I had tested Him before; I put my weight down on Jesus and He was there. He is still there. Men with their threats come and go, but He is permanent. The promises of Christ do not guarantee a soft, easy life without difficulty; they do guarantee against defeat.

The question of the significance of what we are doing concerns many of us in business. We don't want to miss our opportunity in life. Obviously we have not the time, strength, or ability for everything. Some things are harmful, others merely frivolous sidetracks that may be all right for a lark, but not enough for a life purpose. Is what I am doing important?

Jesus said to pray believing and we would receive. Several

years ago I received definite guidance to go after my professional engineering license in a branch of study different from my college major. It took a lot of time and hard work, and I'm still not sure exactly how He wants me to use it, but He will show me as He has each step to date. He has a plan for His whole creation, and we are invited to play a part in it—His specific plan for us. We can know it if we will to know it.

In addition to offering us a place to exercise our specific talents and training, the market is the Christian layman's place of ministry. He has a chance to witness where the clergy ordinarily do not. This doesn't mean that we should intrude when not welcome or be dishonest with the use of company time. But we make contacts with people who have questions and problems, and opportunities to share our faith arise naturally if we are sensitive, considerate, and listening with our inner ear. Trade and professional associations provide opportunities to contribute to the raising of ethical standards.

Finally, as a result of our market place experience, we laymen have much in common with others who work, and this gives us the special "in" of knowledgeability. We can meet with them in fellowship groups within the Church. There are luncheon and breakfast groups for business people under the aegis of Faith at Work, International Christian Leadership, and a number of other organizations and churches. We need the strengthening of His Spirit found in the company of His committed people in the church family, and in vital groups. We can be exposed to the active faith and experience of others. In this we can share what He has given us. Faith is unique in that we must give it away in order to keep it.   —*September, 1964*

Bob Ellis is a true twentieth-century man: bright, capable, efficient. His history of atheism and experimentation is also typical. We can all take heart from the story of Bob and Bunny

Ellis, for they represent an increasing number of laymen who are giving the Church a new thrust in our time. The passing of years has neither slowed them down nor dampened their enthusiasm, for their ministry today in groups and youth work has all the marks of "full steam ahead." They have held out an answer to the anguish not only of individuals but of whole groups, and it seems appropriate to give Bob this challenging last word.